Selected Works

Worcester

Selected Works

Art Museum

Worcester, Massachusetts

This publication is supported by generous grants and gifts from the National Endowment for the Arts, the Fred Harris Daniels Foundation, the Albert W. Rice Charitable Foundation, the Estate of Rose Lincoln Dresser, and John Herron, Jr.

Published by the Worcester Art Museum
55 Salisbury Street
Worcester, Massachusetts 01609

The Worcester Art Museum acknowledges permission to reproduce the following works:
Page 221: *In a Glendale Studio* by Edward Weston. © 1981 Center for Creative Photography, Arizona Board of Regents
Page 229: *Spectre* by Franz Kline. © 1994 Franz Kline/VAGA, New York
Page 231: *Great American Nude* by Tom Wesselmann. © 1994 Tom Wesselmann/VAGA, New York
Page 234: *Lyre* by Kenneth Noland. © 1994 Kenneth Noland/VAGA, New York

Produced by Marquand Books, Inc., Seattle
Printed and bound in Hong Kong

Cover: Paul Gauguin, *The Brooding Woman,* 1891 (p. 149)
Frontispiece: Benjamin West, *Pharaoh and His Host Lost in the Red Sea,* 1792 (detail, p. 184)
Page 19: *Bayezid I, "The Thunderbolt," Routs the Crusaders at the Battle of Nicopolis,* 1584 (detail, p. 65)
Page 67: *The Drinking Contest of Dionysos and Heracles,* about A.D. 100 (detail, p. 81)
Page 85: Pieter Saenredam, *Interior of the Choir of Saint Bavo's Church at Haarlem,* 1660 (detail, p. 125)
Page 165: *Urn with Human Figure,* 300 B.C.–A.D. 200 (detail, p. 168)
Page 177: Edward Hicks, *The Peaceable Kingdom,* about 1833 (detail, p. 195)

Library of Congress Cataloging-in-Publication Data
Worcester Art Museum.
    Selected works from the Worcester Art Museum.
        p.   cm.
    Includes bibliographical references (p. 241) and index.
    1. Art—Massachusetts—Worcester—Catalogs.
  2. Worcester Art Museum—Catalogs.   I. Title.
  N870.A66   1994
    708.144'3—dc20
                                           94-13539
                                             CIP

CONTENTS

6   PREFACE

8   BUILDING A COLLECTION

19   ASIAN ART
21   CHINESE
33   JAPANESE
50   KOREAN
51   INDIAN
60   ISLAMIC

67   ANCIENT ART

85   EUROPEAN ART

165   PRECOLUMBIAN ART

177   AMERICAN ART

239   CATALOGUE AUTHORS

240   BIBLIOGRAPHY

241   INDEX OF ARTISTS, TITLES, AND DONORS

PREFACE

This book—*Selected Works*—features over two hundred masterpieces from the Worcester Art Museum. Arranged by culture and in approximate chronological order, this fully illustrated publication offers a cross section of a collection that spans more than fifty centuries. Worcester's holdings have been formed during the past hundred years almost entirely through community support: both objects and acquisition funds have been donated by extremely generous individuals.

Like the building of the Museum's collection, the production of this book has required the collaboration of many. It is my pleasure to acknowledge the various contributors to and supporters of this publication, which celebrates the achievements of the Museum's family and friends. I am delighted to thank the curatorial staff and outside scholars who helped to select the works of art for publication and drafted the text. We are particularly pleased to have entries written by scholars who have worked with these objects for many years. Susan E. Strickler, Director of Curatorial Affairs, did an excellent job coordinating the preparation and editing of the manuscript. The Scholarship and Publications Committee, chaired successively by trustees Marianne E. Gibson and James N. Heald II, worked with the curators and their colleagues in the Education and Public Affairs departments to develop a format and style that would be both appealing and accessible. Ann McCrea, Director of Publications, ably oversaw the design and production stages. Julia Bailey, Assistant Curator of Indian and Islamic Art at the Sackler Art Museum of Harvard University, graciously provided much of the information on the Islamic objects. We are grateful to Sandra Hachey, former Coordinator of Photographic Services, and to Stephen Briggs, Staff Photographer, for the excellent illustrations. The Registrar's office, headed by Joan-Elisabeth Reid, provided important support to this project. Judy Spear, who served as manuscript editor, deserves special thanks, as does Margaret Avery, who typed the manuscript. I would like to thank Marquand Books, Inc. for the handsome design and efficient production of this catalogue.

Enabling all of this work to be carried out were the generous funders of the project. Once again public and private sources joined in recognition of the Museum's outstanding collections. The Fred Harris Daniels Foundation provided the lead gift to initiate the endeavor. The National Endowment for the Arts awarded two grants supporting manuscript preparation as well as design and production. We are also grateful to the Albert W. Rice Charitable Foundation for support which continues the tradition of Albert and Mary Gage Rice's devotion to the Museum.

John Herron, Jr., made a generous contribution to the project, adding to the gift from the estate of his aunt, Rose Lincoln Dresser. This Worcester family represents the paradigm of devotion to the Museum. Frank Farnum Dresser, the grandfather of Mr. Herron and the father of Miss Dresser, served as a trustee between 1914 and his death in 1924. He undoubtedly instilled a love for this institution in his children, including Louisa Dresser Campbell, who was appointed Associate in Decorative Arts by Francis Henry Taylor in 1932. During a forty-year tenure in which Mrs. Campbell became an eminent scholar of American art, she also served as Acting Director during World War II and subsequently as Curator of Collections. In recognition of the innumerable achievements and contributions of Louisa Dresser Campbell, as well as her lifelong devotion to the institution, the friends and staff of the Worcester Art Museum warmly join me in dedicating *Selected Works* to her memory.

James A. Welu
Director

BUILDING A COLLECTION

On 10 May 1898 the Worcester Art Museum first opened its doors to the public. Through the foresight of its primary founder and benefactor, Stephen Salisbury III, the Museum had been established in 1896 by fifty prominent citizens "solely in trust for the benefit of all the people of the City of Worcester." The group of women and men whom Salisbury had called together in his nearby Greek Revival–style mansion represented a variety of talents from the community—businessmen, lawyers, clergy, artists, and collectors. As the original corporators, they had a lasting effect on the crucial early decades of the Museum's development. They envisioned the institution as a resource for cultural enrichment within a burgeoning industrial city. Today the Worcester Art Museum approaches its centennial as one of New England's largest, with holdings that represent over fifty centuries of art from the great civilizations of both East and West.

During its first decade the Museum's Classical Revival–style building, designed by the Worcester architect Stephen C. Earle, housed relatively modest collections—mostly plaster casts of sculpture from the ancient and Renaissance worlds and works of art on loan. While the daily administration was overseen by a manager, John Green Heywood, the trustees took charge of acquiring works of art and mounting exhibitions.

The Museum's first important acquisitions came from bequests. In 1901 John Chandler Bancroft—a wealthy Bostonian whose grandfather had been a Unitarian minister in Worcester—bequeathed a group of over three thousand Japanese prints. The Bancroft collection spans the history of woodcut print-making in Japan, with particular strength in rare, early images from the late seventeenth and eighteenth century. In 1906 Bancroft's widow bequeathed his Japanese paintings, as well as acquisition funds that have enabled successive Museum staff to build upon these rich holdings.

Less than a decade after he founded the Museum, Stephen Salisbury III died. A bachelor with diverse business interests and large real-estate holdings, Salisbury was Worcester's wealthiest benefactor. His death in 1905 marked the end of an influential family, who had come to Worcester just prior to the Revolution. Salisbury's bequest included many portraits commissioned by his family, as well as sculpture, furniture, and silver acquired by his parents and grandparents. These works—by such artists as Gilbert Stuart, Thomas Crawford, and Samuel F. B. Morse and the craftsmen Edward Winslow, Paul Revere, and Nathaniel Hurd—constituted the nucleus of the American collections, an area that would ultimately become an acknowledged strength. Salisbury's legacy also included a bequest of over $3 million—an enormous sum at the time—which set the fledgling institution on firm financial footing.

Portrait of Stephen Salisbury III, 1891, by Frederick Porter Vinton (1864–1911),
American, oil on canvas, 50 × 40 in. (127 × 101.6 cm). Bequest of Stephen
Salisbury III, 1907.31.

Worcester Art Museum, 1896, an architectural rendering by George C. Halcott (?–1930), American, watercolor over graphite on paper, 15¾ × 24⅛ in. (40 × 61.2 cm). Bequest of Stephen Salisbury III, 1907.86.

With the arrival in November 1908 of its first professional director, Philip J. Gentner, the Museum began to develop its collections more aggressively. A man with broad interests, Gentner made acquisitions in many areas during his ten-year directorship. In 1909 the Museum purchased three thousand American prints from the private holdings of Charles E. Goodspeed, whose family had operated Boston's oldest and most prestigious shop for historical prints and illustrated books. This acquisition—including sheets by such notables as Peter Pelham, Paul Revere, and Amos Doolittle—laid the foundation for Worcester's strong holdings in American prints. Gentner bought a number of important colonial paintings by John Singleton Copley, Joseph Blackburn, and Ralph Earl, as well as canvases by American Impressionists like Frank Benson, Edmund Tarbell, and Childe Hassam, all of whom who exhibited in the Museum's annual exhibitions of contemporary art mounted between 1898 and 1912. Recognizing the powerful expression of the works in watercolor by Winslow Homer and John Singer Sargent, Gentner competed against larger institutions to purchase significant groups by these two great American masters. He expanded the modest ancient collections, acquiring a series of important Roman portrait heads dating from the first through the third century A.D. Gentner also made strong acquisitions in European painting, including Italian works by Stefano da Verona, Pesellino, and Giovanni Battista Moroni; major eighteenth-century British portraits by William Hogarth and Thomas Gainsborough; and two canvases by the French Impressionist Claude Monet.

In an effort to build the Museum's holdings systematically, Gentner's successors in the 1920s acquired the cornerstones of the medieval collection.

Interior of the Worcester Art Museum, about 1910.

Raymond Henniker-Heaton (né Raymond Wyer) purchased in 1924 the imposing late thirteenth-century wall frescoes from the Italian church of Santa
Maria inter Angelos near Spoleto. The church building had been previously
secularized and incorporated into a working farm, from which the preserved
frescoes were removed not long before Henniker-Heaton convinced the trustees to acquire them. In 1927 George Eggers purchased the twelfth-century
French chapter house that had been originally part of the Benedictine priory
of Saint John at Le Bas-Nueil near Poitiers. Its installation in 1932 in the
Museum's major new addition, which houses the Renaissance Court, attracted that year over two hundred thousand visitors, who came to see this
early reconstruction of Romanesque architecture within an American museum setting.

     Henniker-Heaton also added key European paintings, including several
Spanish works by Alonso Cano, Jusepe de Ribera, and El Greco. He also purchased *The Brooding Woman,* one of the first paintings by Paul Gauguin to
enter an American museum. Eggers was director when, in 1926, Mrs. Kingsmill Marrs of Boston bequeathed over two thousand prints, a gift that essentially established Worcester's collection of old-master prints. Under the
tutelage of Sylvester Rosa Kohler—the pioneering curator of graphic arts
at the Museum of Fine Arts in Boston—Mrs. Marrs had built a strong representation of the history of color printmaking from the Renaissance through
the nineteenth century. The Marrs bequest—still the single most important
gift to Worcester's print collection—included such diverse and extraordinary
treasures as chiaroscuro woodcuts by Ugo da Carpi and Hendrik Goltzius and
a complete set of ten color intaglio prints by the Impressionist Mary Cassatt.

Installation of the Antioch mosaics in the Renaissance Court, about 1937.

Though more inclusive than color prints, the Marrs Collection established an emphasis that has been expanded over the intervening fifty years, both through acquisitions by curators and by the many generous gifts of twentieth-century American color prints from Mr. and Mrs. James N. Heald II.

The 1930s proved to be an exciting decade under the first of two tenures of the director Francis Henry Taylor. Building on the strong foundation of his predecessors, Taylor revealed through the diversity of his acquisitions a conscious effort to develop collections reflecting a consistent outline of the history of art. In the field of antiquities he added an outstanding Assyrian relief, several Egyptian sculptures, and the fourth-century B.C. Greek stele depicting an old man. Upon his return to Worcester in the 1950s, Taylor purchased an important late sixth-century B.C. Greek amphora attributed to the Rycroft Painter.

Unequivocally Worcester's greatest ancient treasures, a group of Roman mosaics dating from the first through the sixth century A.D.—excavated at Antioch in Syria—was unveiled in the Renaissance Court of the new building during Taylor's first directorship. The Worcester Art Museum had supported this excavation between 1932 and 1939 in partnership with the Baltimore Art Museum, Princeton University, Wellesley College, Dumbarton Oaks, and the National Museums of France. Consequently Worcester now holds one of the finest collections of Roman mosaics in America.

Taylor also acquired in the 1930s excellent Indian and Persian paintings with support from the Worcester lawyer and museum trustee Alexander H. Bullock. Upon his death in 1962, Bullock not only bequeathed his private collection but also provided a significant endowment designated for Asian art. Taylor inspired others to collect, among them Aldus C. Higgins, who acquired paintings and sculpture by Georges Braque, Wassily Kandinsky, Georges Rouault, and Jacques Lipchitz. Higgins bequeathed these works to the Museum and significantly strengthened the core holdings of European modern art. In the area of old-master painting Taylor purchased such cornerstone works of the fifteenth and sixteenth centuries as *The Discovery of Honey by Bacchus* by Piero di Cosimo, *The Rest on the Flight into Egypt* by Quentin Massys, *The Christ of Saint Gregory* by an unknown Provençal master, and a rare portrait of a woman at her toilette from the School of Fontainebleau. During these same years Taylor bought the Museum's first and most significant tapestry, *The Last Judgement,* designed by a Flemish artist of the late fifteenth century and woven in Brussels.

The single most important gift of European and American paintings came in 1940 through the bequest of Mary G. Ellis. She and her husband, Theodore T. Ellis, a successful newspaper publisher and industrialist, had collected in their Worcester home a substantial group of paintings. The Ellis Collection comprises examples in almost every school from the late fourteenth to the mid-nineteenth century, including paintings by Carlo Crivelli, Lorenzo di Credi, Niccolò di Bartolomeo Pisano, Jacob van Ruisdael, Hubert Robert, Jean-Honoré Fragonard, and J. M. W. Turner. English and French porcelains and furniture from the Ellis home were also part of the bequest, as were significant American paintings by Winslow Homer, James Abbott McNeill Whistler, Childe Hassam, Ralph Blakelock, and Albert Pinkham Ryder. A newly appointed director, Charles H. Sawyer, had just arrived in Worcester to welcome this magnificent gift. Developing the paintings collection still further, Sawyer purchased some stunning European and American canvases, including works by the Baroque master Bernardo Strozzi, the French Rococo artist Jean-Baptiste Pater, and the American modernist Marsden Hartley.

Sawyer also directed in 1943 the opening of the first gallery devoted to Precolumbian art, establishing the Museum as a leader in the exhibition of these objects as works of art rather than as anthropological or archaeological specimens. Kester D. Jewell, who had been trained at the Newark Museum, was appointed curator of Precolumbian art in 1946. During the next twenty-five years he oversaw the systematic development of this small holding, which has grown to be the second largest of its kind in New England. Today it offers a comprehensive survey of cultures that thrived in Central and South America prior to the Spanish Conquest in the early sixteenth century, from such present-day regions as Mexico, Guatemala, Costa Rica, Colombia, and Peru. This collection was greatly enriched by the Worcester patrons Aldus C. Higgins, a trustee and Museum president, and Charles B. Cohn and Stuart P. Anderson, devoted collectors and teachers.

The pioneering conservator George Stout succeeded Charles Sawyer as director in 1947. Stout bought several key seventeenth-century Dutch paintings, most notably *Banquet Still Life* by Abraham van Beyeren, *The Rhetoricians* by Jan Steen, *Winter Landscape with Skaters near a Castle* by Adriaen van de Venne, and *Interior of the Choir of Saint Bavo's Church at Haarlem* by Pieter Saenredam. He also ventured into the field of European drawings,

A view into the American galleries, 1993.

an area in which the Museum had previously collected only sporadically. During his second tenure at Worcester—following his fifteen-year directorship at the Metropolitan Museum of Art in New York—Francis Henry Taylor built upon Stout's initiative, adding in 1956 eighteen important old-master drawings, which formed the nucleus of a holding that now numbers over fifteen hundred sheets. Taylor's acquisitions included chiefly Italian, French, and Flemish drawings dating from the sixteenth through the eighteenth century by Stefano della Bella, Giovanni Benedetto Castiglione, Guercino, and Parmigianino.

During the late 1950s and 1960s Taylor's successor, Daniel Catton Rich, consciously carried forward the policy of his predecessors to strengthen the permanent collections in several areas, rather than to specialize in any one field. Rich's acquisitions of European paintings by Gerrit van Honthorst, Jean-Baptiste Greuze, Jean-Baptiste Oudry, Sir Thomas Lawrence, and James Tissot reveal his broad tastes. He also took advantage of opportunities in Asian art in the post–World War II era, making significant acquisitions in Japanese and Chinese painting, Indian sculpture, and Chinese ceramics. His most distinguished purchase in the Asian field is the eleven-headed Kannon, which stands today as one of the most important Heian-period sculptures outside of Japan.

Rich was devoted to art of the twentieth century. He not only organized a groundbreaking exhibition of Pop Art, but he also purchased paintings by contemporary artists Tom Wesselmann and Ellsworth Kelly. At a time when few art museums recognized photography as a fine art, Rich provided, in

A view into the Precolumbian galleries, 1994.

1962, the leadership to begin a collection, an initiative he had undertaken during his earlier tenure as director of the Art Institute of Chicago. Among the first acquisitions in this field were photographs by Ansel Adams, Harry Callahan, Arnold Newman, Andreas Feininger, and Todd Webb. In 1962 Rich appointed as curator of photography Stephen B. Jareckie, who has since acquired over 1800 works—examples that all together survey the 150-year history of this medium in Europe and America. Rich was a source of encouragement to many collectors like Chapin Riley, whose gifts of paintings and drawings by Vincent van Gogh, Pierre-Auguste Renoir, Paul Signac, and Charles Burchfield have filled out the Museum's holdings of early twentieth-century art.

During Rich's tenure a pair of portraits—Worcester's two most famous American works—were added to the collection. Owing in large part to the long-time efforts of Louisa Dresser Campbell, curator of the collections and a distinguished historian of American art, the pendant portraits—*Mrs. Elizabeth Freake and Baby Mary* and *John Freake*—were acquired from descendants of the sitters. The generosity of Albert W. and Mary G. Rice enabled Worcester to keep these icons of seventeenth-century New England in Massachusetts, where they had been since they were painted in 1671. Today they are the centerpieces of strong holdings of colonial and Federal portraiture that Mrs. Campbell helped to develop during her forty years on the curatorial staff.

In 1970 Richard Stuart Teitz, a former Ford Fellow at Worcester, succeeded his mentor, Daniel Catton Rich, as director. A classicist, Teitz as a fellow had recommended to Rich the acquisition of the exquisite bronze portrait bust of

An aerial view of the Worcester Art Museum, 1992.

a Roman lady dating from the second century A.D. As director he acquired a number of important Italian, French, and Dutch Baroque paintings, including Hyacinthe Rigaud's *Marquis de Louville*. In 1980 the chief curator, James A. Welu, engendered great excitement in the community announcing his discovery of a painting by Andrea del Sarto that had gone unrecognized for many years; *Saint John the Baptist*, is one of only a few works by this High Renaissance master in America. Probably brought to this country in the mid-nineteenth century by the Brooks family of Boston, *Saint John* traveled through inheritance to Worcester with Harriett Brooks Hawkins, who gave the painting to All Saints Church in 1959. After the attribution to Sarto was substantiated, the Worcester community rallied together, making possible the Museum's acquisition of this rare work in 1984.

Like Rich, Teitz had a strong interest in late twentieth-century art, and under his leadership several important works on paper by leading artists—Jasper Johns, Frank Stella, Sol Lewitt, Roy Lichtenstein, and Robert Rauschenberg—were purchased through funds from the National Endowment for the Arts. During the late 1970s William and Saundra Lane presented many paintings, drawings, and photographs by key figures, including Charles Sheeler, Morris Graves, Mark Tobey, Hans Hofmann, Franz Kline, and Milton Avery. Some of the most outstanding gifts of contemporary prints and drawings came from Sidney and Rosalie Rose and their family during the tenure of Teitz's successor, Tom L. Freudenheim, in the early 1980s. Works by David Hockney, Alex Katz, Robert Rauschenberg, and Frank Stella from the Rose

Collection significantly amplified the representation of leading movements and figures on the contemporary scene.

Both Teitz and Freudenheim enlarged the curatorial staff, shaping it to serve the strengths of growing collections as well as expanded activities related to acquisitions, scholarship, and exhibitions. In the 1970s and early 1980s, curatorial positions were designated in prints and drawings, European art, American art, and Asian art. In 1990 the first full-time curatorship in contemporary art was established by the current director, James A. Welu.

Appointed director in 1985, Welu has continued to develop the Dutch and Flemish seventeenth-century holdings, chiefly through generous gifts from the Worcester community. Particularly noteworthy are works from the collection of John and Ruth Adam by Paul Brill, Jan Cossiers, and Pieter Lastman; from Milton and Alice Higgins, a Pieter Brueghel the Younger; and from Robert and Mary S. Cushman, a Judith Leyster.

Throughout the 96-year history of the Museum, the Worcester community has been its strongest supporter. The contributions of many Worcester families have resulted not only in gifts of artwork but in acquisition funds and critical operational support. Today funds bearing the names of Charlotte E. W. Buffington, Alexander H. Bullock, Theodore T. and Mary G. Ellis, Austin S. and Sarah C. Garver, and Eliza S. Paine represent the farsighted generosity of many of the Museum's early benefactors. In the late 1970s the Stoddard family, who for decades had supported the Museum anonymously, made a gift that more than doubled the endowment for acquiring works of art. The Stoddard Acquisition Fund has enabled directors and curators to maintain the high standards set by their predecessors as they develop the collections. In highlighting some of Worcester's great masterpieces, this handbook stands as a tribute to the long-standing partnership between the Museum and its community that the founders envisioned almost a century ago "for the benefit of all."

Susan E. Strickler
Director of Curatorial Affairs
Curator of American Art

Asian Art

Ritual Wine Container (Fang I)
    15th–13th century B.C.
    Chinese, Shang dynasty
    Bronze
    H: 6½ in. (16.4 cm) W: 4½ in. (11.4 cm)
    D: 3⅟₁₆ in. (7.8 cm)
    Inscribed inside with two characters
    Museum purchase, 1952.7

By the end of China's Bronze Age, sophisticated vessels were made for preparing and serving sacrificial food and wine. As the most precious possessions—emblems of sovereignty, prestige, wealth, and power—such bronzes were buried with the dead. The clarity of design and architectonic shape of this ritual wine container result from the uniquely Chinese piece-mold method of casting that produced it. After the design was carved in reverse into clay molds, molten metal was poured into the assembled sections. The bronze worker exploited the technique for artistic ends to produce in the finished work finely wrought ornament and three-dimensional ridges cast by the joins between the mold sections that retain an overall segmented effect. Bilaterally symmetrical masklike designs with protruding eyes (*taotie*), the dominant Shang decorative motif, appear on each side of the vessel and the front and back of its roof. Birds, snakes, and a squared spiral (*lei wen*) covering the ground complete the decor. The container's use in ritual suggests that its ornamentation had meaning, but no specific interpretation can be advanced. The inscription is probably a clan name.   —EdeSS

Ritual Wine Container (Yu)
    11th century B.C.
    Chinese, Shang dynasty
    Bronze
    H: 9⅞ in. (24 cm) W: 6¹¹⁄₁₆ in. (17 cm)
    D: 6 in. (15 cm)
    Inscribed inside with one character
    Museum purchase, 1940.18

This *yu*, or lidded wine jar, is a splendid example of the Shang bronze caster's art. Both
lid and body are richly ornamented with a
band of vertical ribbing, which contrasts with
the densely patterned horizontal bands of
stylized birds on a ground of squared spiral
whorls (*lei wen*). The mold joins that divide
the vessel into quarters have been exploited to
give the container its spiky, expressive silhouette. Three-dimensional animal heads decorate

the ends of its swinging handle. The exquisite
patina, valued highly by collectors and con-
noisseurs, is not an intentional artistic effect
but accidental, resulting from the interaction
of the copper in the bronze with moisture
during the vessel's years buried underground
in a tomb. The one-character inscription is
probably a clan name.

Bronzes like this one are the primary
sources of information on ancient China. The
production of vessels of such sophistication
implies the existence of wealth, highly developed bronze technology, and a ritual system.

—EdeSS

Ritual Wine Container (Lei)
    8th–7th century B.C.
    Chinese, Eastern Zhou dynasty
    Bronze
    H: 10⅞ in. (27.3 cm) DIAM: 12¼ in. (31 cm)
    Gift of Mrs. F. Harold Daniels, 1957.1

With loop handles cast onto its wide shoulders and a broad, everted mouth rim, this flat-bottomed ritual bronze vessel is thought to have held wine. Its shape evolved from that of pottery in the late Western Zhou period (1111–770 B.C.). The decoration, organized in two bands of large, interlocking dragons, heralds a change in taste in the early Eastern Zhou dynasty. In the following centuries such designs became denser and more regular in their arrangement of complex, repeated abstract patterns. That the decoration may not have had specific symbolic meaning can be inferred from inscriptions on some Zhou bronzes indicating that they commemorated military victories and gifts of land or titles.

—EdeSS

Ritual Wine Container (Hu)
1st century B.C.–1st century A.D.
Chinese, Han dynasty
Earthenware painted in green and red
H: 15⅜ in. (39 cm) DIAM: 10⅞ in. (27.5 cm)
Alexander H. Bullock Fund and Sarah C.
Garver Fund, 1991.36

During the second and first centuries B.C.,
the wealth and cosmopolitanism of the Han
dynasty produced a flowering of the arts:
exquisite objects were made both for decoration and for religious or ritual use. Members
of the imperial clan, as well as newly rich
merchants, officials, and landowners, created
a demand for elaborate burial paraphernalia
that glorified filial piety. This pottery *hu* is
an example of such funerary wares.

Elegantly proportioned and painted in
fluid, linear designs, the jar imitates in shape
and decoration the more expensive lacquer
and inlaid-bronze vessels of the late War-
ring States (475–221 B.C.) and Western Han
(206 B.C.–A.D. 9) periods. Dynamic interlaced
pointed and knobbed scrolls circle the body
in two wide friezes. The domed lid is painted
with abstract motifs that seem to derive from
taotie (animal masks).   —EdeSS

Seated Buddha with Attending Bodhisattvas

> early 6th century A.D.
> Chinese (Shenxi Province), Northern Wei dynasty
> Limestone with polychrome
> H: 55 $\frac{13}{16}$ in. (141.7 cm) W: 39 $\frac{9}{16}$ (100.3 cm)
> D: 12 $\frac{5}{8}$ in. (32 cm)
> Museum purchase, 1934.34

On the front of this stele Shakyamuni, the historical Buddha, is flanked by bodhisattvas, deities who have put off their own enlightenment in order to help mankind attain salvation. The back, which lacks a systematic symbolic or narrative program, is dominated by a large standing "universal" Buddha, also attended by bodhisattvas, raising his hand in the gesture of reassurance. Three seated Buddhas in the halo symbolize the deity's eternal nature, a concept that gained importance in China in the fifth century A.D. Scenes of the life of the historical Buddha and related legends cover the remaining surface. The imagery of the entire stele is standard for Mahayana, the dominant sect of East Asian Buddhism, which preaches a doctrine of universal salvation through numerous bodhisattvas. The didactic content of this sculpture would have reached the faithful who saw it in its original temple context.

The linear carving is distinctly Chinese in contrast to the volumetric forms of the Indian sculpture from which the imagery derives. Long, narrow heads, attenuated bodies, and linear surface rhythms reveal a stylistic relationship with the metropolitan style of the Northern Wei period. A strong provincial character is expressed, however, in the parallel lines of the flattened drapery folds and the awkward body proportions. The red and blue paint remaining over large areas of the front of this sculpture demonstrates that color was an essential part of its visual impact.

—EDESS

Head of a Buddha

A.D. 550–77
Chinese (Henan Province), Northern
Qi dynasty
Limestone
H: 17½ in. (44.5 cm) W: 10⅝ in. (27 cm)
D: 13⁷⁄₁₆ in. (34 cm)
Museum purchase, 1914.24

In the middle of the sixth century A.D., many Indians and Persians were living in China, and Turks, who traveled on horseback through Central Asia to Persia (modern Iran), were in power north of the Great Wall. These influences transformed the figures at the enormous complex of Buddhist cave temples at North Xiangtang Shan from the linear abstraction of the Northern Wei style to a more rounded, three-dimensional one. This head may have belonged to a seated image of the Buddha. An almost geometric simplicity differentiates the sculpture from its Indian and Central Asian sources. The crisp, direct carving and almost mathematical perfection of this work are characteristic of images remaining at the site.   —EdeSS

Mirror
　　　late 7th or early 8th century A.D.
　　　Chinese, Tang dynasty
　　　Gilt bronze
　　　DIAM: 5⅜ in. (13.7 cm)
　　　Jerome Wheelock Fund, 1955.12

The consolidation of power and wealth in the seventh and early eighth centuries A.D. made the era of the Tang dynasty (A.D. 618–about 907) one of the richest periods in Chinese cultural history. Its brilliant, cosmopolitan character is reflected in the arts as people, ideas, and exotica came to its capital, Changan, from all over Asia. A popular Tang dynasty motif was the lion-and-grapevine design shown here, carrying associations that were traditional for Chinese mirror-back decoration: the harmony of the universe and the balance of the forces of nature. It was during the preceding Sui dynasty (A.D. 581–618) that the Chinese had borrowed the grapevine motif from Sassanian Persian silver and textiles. Also in the Sui dynasty lions replaced the indigenous Chinese decor of dragons, zodiac animals, and other cosmological symbols, appearing as fierce, strong beasts of good omen. A new Tang interpretation made the lion a playful creature and added three dimensionality and high relief to the design.

—EdeSS

UNIDENTIFIED COURT PAINTER

Chinese, Ming dynasty
*Ming Huang and Yang Gueifei Listening
to Music,* 1368–1400
Handscroll; ink and light color on silk
11⅞ × 51⅞ in. (30.1 × 131.8 cm)
Seals: three interpolated seals of Qian Xuan
(about 1235–after 1300)
Museum purchase, 1936.4

The great Tang emperor Ming Huang (reigned
A.D. 712–56) was an outstanding patron of the
arts, and music flourished at his court. This
subject—women orchestral musicians playing for the emperor and his concubine Yang
Gueifei—is known in several versions that
go back from Ming through Song (A.D. 960–
1279) to a famous Tang (A.D. 618–about 907)
painting, or a Five Dynasties (A.D. 907–60)
prototype (now lost). The work illustrated
here, which recalls the painting of the Yuan
dynasty (about 1280–1368) court, has features that signal a new interpretation of an
older style: sophisticated poses, complex re-
lationships between figures, exquisite calligraphic drawing, and harmonious colors. Three
seals affixed to the end of the scene, attributed
to Qian Xuan, are modern additions.

—EdeSS

Bottle-shaped Vase
early 15th century
Chinese, Ming dynasty
Porcelain with underglaze-blue decoration
H: 17 1/16 in. (43.3 cm)
DIAM: 13 5/8 in. (34.6 cm)
Museum purchase, 1959.6

In their importance to Chinese culture, ceramics are comparable to secular sculpture in the West. The most influential ceramic type in history, Ming underglaze-blue decorated porcelain was exported from China to Southeast Asia and to Europe and was carried in Arab ships throughout the Islamic world. This vase, painted all over with peonies in a leafy scroll, is characteristic of the outstanding blue-and-white ceramics manufactured under imperial patronage at the Jingdezhen kilns in the early Ming dynasty. Its quality identifies it as an object created for refined Chinese taste and not for export.

In addition to the painting, which shows great sensitivity in line and shading, the technical process contributed to the depth and richness of the surface. Sometime during firing, the cobalt blue pigment "heaped and piled," creating small, dark dots; at other times the pigment ran. Both of these accidental circumstances enliven the piece with tonal variations and painterly effects.   —EdeSS

WEN ZHENGMING

Chinese, 1470–1559
Bamboo, Orchids, Rock, and Calligraphy,
about 1530
Handscroll; ink on paper
11⅜ × 47¼ in. (28.5 × 119.5 cm)
Signature: seals of the artist in inscription
Seals: (upper) Wen Zhengming yin,
(lower) Zheng-Zhung
Charlotte E. W. Buffington Fund, 1960.10

Wen Zhengming was one of the leading artists of the Wu school, the scholar-painters who carried on the amateur tradition in Chinese painting during the Ming dynasty (1368–1644). Having had an official career in the Hanlin Academy in Beijing, he retired early to his native city of Suzhou, a cultivated intellectual center. There, having access to original works by the great painters of the past in private collections, Wen Zhengming became an outstanding critic and connoisseur of painting. Although his notion of style was bound to the canons governing forms and motifs laid down by past masters, this did not prevent him from introducing invention and change in his own work.

This painting is an example of the artist's mature style of the 1530s. A superb calligrapher as well as a painter, Wen Zhengming wrote in his own hand the poems on the scroll. Both the calligraphic text and the painting suggest that subject matter was a pretext for exploring formal concerns and technique. The orchid and the bamboo—understood as moralizing symbols in earlier periods—had lost their metaphorical content by the sixteenth century.

—EdeSS

DING YUNPENG

Chinese, active 1584–1638
Landscape with Figures under a Tree, 1616
Fan painting; ink and gold leaf on paper
7 1/16 × 22 3/8 in. (17.9 × 51.7 cm)
Signature: Ding Yunpeng
Seals: one of the artist and two of collectors
Museum purchase, 1960.11

Ding Yunpeng, who lived for some time in a Chan (Zen) Buddhist temple, was admired by contemporaries as a fine literati (scholar-official) painter. He was involved with the intellectual circle of the great Ming artist and critic Dong Qichang, and his use of ink tone and textured rock surfaces in the landscape recalls the broad, wet brushwork of Shen Zhou, the first great painter of the influential Wu school, the mainstream of Ming literati painting. Working in the literati tradition of monochrome drawing, Ding painted radically abstracted natural forms with greater intellectual than sensory appeal.

This tiny masterpiece reflects the artist's work as a designer for woodblocks. Rather than depicting illusory space, Ding aimed for powerful surface design: an interplay of textures and patterns massed as coherent units across the fan.   —EdeSS

DAO JI (SHITAO)
Chinese, 1642–1708
Autumn Landscape, 1701
Hanging scroll; ink and color on paper
76⅜ × 29¾ in. (194 × 75.5 cm)
Signatures: Zing-Xiang chen ren, Dadizu, and Shitao
Seals: five of the artist, two of the collector Ouyang Lin dated 1907, three of collectors in lower left, and four in lower right corner
Charlotte E. W. Buffington Fund, 1960.9

An eminent theorist on art, well schooled in the painting of the past, Dao Ji (also known as Shitao) became the greatest of all Qing period (about 1644–1912) artists. In an era of strict allegiance to earlier styles, this independent artist abandoned established traditions and developed methods from the interaction with his own place and time. His declaration that he followed no style was revolutionary for the historically minded Chinese.

While this work lacks the balance and control of Dao Ji's works of the 1680s and 1690s, it shows an exemplary willingness to take risks, even late in life. Also an outstanding calligrapher, Dao Ji referred to the creation of the painting and the poem that inspired it in the expressive and elegant inscription at the upper right.   —EdeSS

Juichimen Kannon
(eleven-headed Kannon)
> early 10th century A.D.
> Japanese, Heian period
> Solid woodblock construction with traces
> of polychrome
> H: 67 in. (170.4 cm) W: 19¾ in. (50.1 cm)
> D: 15⅝ in. (39.7 cm)
> Eliza S. Paine Fund, 1959.72

Kannon, a symbol of Buddhist wisdom and
compassion, is a bodhisattva, or an enlightened deity who is said to remain in this world
to help mankind find salvation. Some two
hundred years after the introduction of Buddhism to Japan from the Asian mainland in
the mid-sixth century A.D., sculpture developed in response to the doctrinal needs of
the many sects that spread throughout the
country. The eleven-headed Kannon became
the focus of a major cult when, as part of the
popularization of the faith, rites of repen-
tance were carried out before images of this
type. Kannon is associated with the worship
of Amida Buddha, whose image stands in
front of the small heads on the statue.

   Both hands of the bodhisattva are missing; the left one may have made a gesture
of devotion, while the right held a vase with
a lotus, an attribute of this deity. Although
it was meant to be seen frontally, standing
on an altar platform, the sculpture is carved
in the round. Fashioned primarily from a
single large log, the figure was hollowed out
slightly to hold polished stones—symbolic
relics of the Buddha—and documents con-
cerning the history of the piece. The image
is like sculptures of the early Heian period
(A.D. 794–894) in its somber, heavy proportions, frontal symmetry, and simplified anatomy and drapery.   —EDeSS

Head of a Guardian
second half of 11th century
Japanese, Heian period
Assembled woodblock construction with
traces of polychrome and gilding
H: 12¼ in. (31.7 cm) W: 10⅛ in. (25.7 cm)
D: 8³⁄₁₆ in. (20.8 cm)
Museum purchase, 1921.183

The equipoise of this head derives from the
works of the great sculptor Jocho, whose style
dominated Japanese sculpture in the eleventh
century. Reflecting the aristocratic taste of
the Heian capital (modern Kyoto) during the
Fujiwara regency and the flowering of a Japanese cultural and artistic expression, this elegant piece contrasts with the more emphatically Chinese character of ninth-century
Heian sculpture.

Because it is a fragment and no specific
attribute is present, the exact identity of the
head remains unknown. It may have been
from a set of Buddhist guardians of the four
cardinal directions (*Shitenno*) or one of the
twelve heavenly generals (*Juni shinsho*). The
head was once painted and gilded, heightening
the wrathful expression of this protector of
the faith. Its assembled woodblock construction was developed to meet the demand for
images created by the increased patronage of
the Fujiwara period. Using this method, artistic workshops could produce large quantities
of lightweight images with speed, pegging and
gluing together relatively shallowly carved
pieces of wood.   —EdeSS

UNIDENTIFIED KANO SCHOOL PAINTER

Japanese, active 1596–1614
Falcon on Oak Tree Watching Monkeys
Six-panel folding screen; ink and light color on paper
60½ × 126¹⁵⁄₁₆ in. (153.6 × 322.4 cm)
No signature; interpolated jar-shaped *kuninobu* seal of Kano Eitoku (1543–90)
Alexander H. Bullock Fund and Stoddard Acquisition Fund, 1991.172

This screen was created by a member of a school of painters that traces its origins to the fifteenth century and the beginning of ink painting in Japan. Both the emphasis on the foreground and the powerful brushwork identify the artist as someone working in the circle of Kano Sanraku in the Keicho era (1596–1614). Linked to the patronage of the military class and under the leadership of great artists such as Motonobu and Eitoku, Kano school artists invented a vital style associated with a corpus of themes.

The proud, fierce falcon here is heroic in spirit, evoking the ethos of the samurai class; the use of vacant space in an expansive setting dramatizes the conception. *Falcon on Oak Tree* was originally the left-hand screen of a pair. The right one, known only through a photograph, depicted an eagle catching a rabbit.

—EdeSS

ANONYMOUS TOWN PAINTER

Japanese, active early 17th century
Willows by the Uji Bridge
Pair of six-panel folding screens; ink, color,
and gold on paper
(a) 60¾ × 128⅝ in. (154.2 × 323.7 cm)
(b) 60⅞ × 128⁹⁄₁₆ in. (154.4 × 323.6 cm)
Alexander H. Bullock Fund, 1969.110a, b

Providing ready-made pictures for a growing group of affluent townsmen who dominated Edo period (1600–1868) Japan, anonymous painters (*machi-eshi*) carried on the
earlier native Japanese tradition (*yamato-e*)
in themes such as genre, history, the seasons,
and famous places. Their formal language
derived from Japanese sixteenth-century
painting, which was inspired in turn by both
Chinese ink painting and Japanese narrative
painting. The works they created were meant
to please patrons and were devoid of philosophical or moralizing content.

These screens belong to a canonical group of pictures of famous places (*meisho-e*) expressing a distinctive Japanese sensibility—an emotional response to sites renowned for their beauty, particularly when combined with the imagery of the changing seasons. The willows and Uji Bridge theme assumed the form seen here in the Momoyama period (1573–1615)—the great age of screen painting—when gold was used lavishly and dynamic asymmetrical composition produced the simplified close-up view. As a seasonal reference, the passage of time is implied by the changing size of the willow leaves as the viewer moves from right to left through the painting. Realism as well as decoration inspired the three-dimensional treatment of the silvered metal moon, now tarnished, and of water wheels and baskets built up in gesso.

—EdeSS

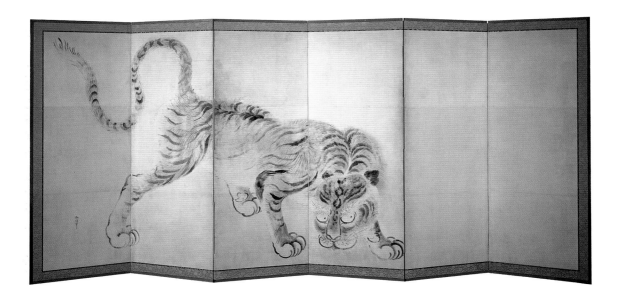

KANO NAONOBU
Japanese, 1607–50
Tiger
Left of a pair of six-panel folding screens;
ink on paper
68 × 149 in. (172.8 × 378.4 cm)
Signature: Naonobu hitsu
Seal: Fujiwara
Harriet B. Bancroft Fund and partial gift
of Robert H. Simmons, 1987.9

The most prolific and versatile painter of the
early Edo period, Kano Tan'yu was deeply
involved in traditional ink painting both as
artist and as connoisseur. As official painter
of the Tokugawa shogunate, Tan'yu had access
to original Chinese Southern Song and Yuan
landscapes, Ming bird-and-flower painting,
and earlier Japanese painting in the Tokugawa
collection. Continuing the ink-painting tradition introduced into Japan from China in the
Muromachi period (1392–1568), the works
of both Tan'yu and his brother Naonobu rep-

resent a new synthesis that drew on all the styles of Japanese painting. The artists' grandfather was the great Kano Eitoku, whose fluent and spontaneous brushwork and spatial organization are echoed in these screens.

The tiger and dragon, old motifs in East Asian art, were adopted into Zen painting as symbols of Buddhist doctrine. The dual subject, which had appealed also to the warlords of the Momoyama period (1573–1615), continued to be popular with artists through the eighteenth century.　　　　　—EdeSS

KANO TAN'YU
Japanese, 1602–74
Dragon
Right of a pair of six-panel folding screens; ink on paper
68 × 149 in. (172.8 × 378.4 cm)
No signature
Seal: Uneme
Harriet B. Bancroft Fund and partial gift of Robert H. Simmons, 1987.10

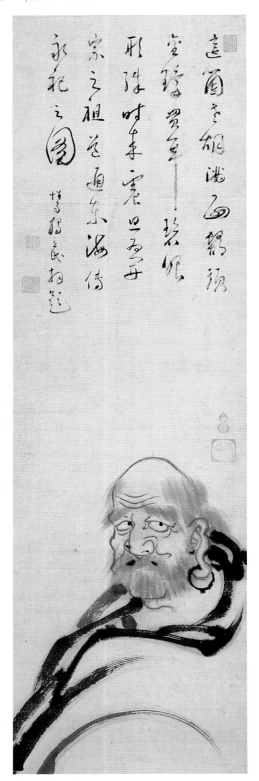

OBAKU DOKURYU (Calligrapher)
Japanese, 1596–1672
Painting traditionally attributed to
Unkoku Toeki, 1591–1644
Daruma
Hanging scroll; ink on paper
39⅞ × 11¾ in. (98.7 × 29.8 cm)
Signature: Shoeki Dokuryu shi Haidai
Seals: (upper) Dokuryu, (lower) Tengai
Ichikanjin
Alexander H. Bullock Fund, 1983.32

This painting of Daruma (Bodhidharma), the
Indian monk who traveled to China in the
sixth century A.D. and founded Zen Buddhism,
has a traditional attribution to Unkoku Toeki
on the basis of seals probably added at a later
date. The calligraphy is of greater interest
than the portrait, with which it shares a
highly simplified style.

Dokuryu (Chinese: Tai Li) was a Chinese
scholar and calligrapher who fled the Manchu
conquest of his homeland and arrived in Japan
in 1653. He took the name Dokuryu when
he became a monk under Ingen, the Chinese
founder of Mampukuji, the Obaku Zen temple
near Kyoto. The Obaku sect was influential in
the spread of contemporary Chinese culture
in Japan during the Edo period (1600–1868).

Dokuryu's cursive script shares characteristics with his Chinese contemporaries in
the late Ming period and has a freedom and
rhythm entirely its own, distinct from the
calligraphic style of other Obaku Zen monk-
calligraphers. The fluid brushwork seen here,
with its contrast of wet and dry, light and
dark ink, captures the typically irreverent
Zen spirit of the inscription, which calls the
subject (Daruma) "the old clot."   —EdeSS

TORII KIYONOBU I

Japanese, about 1664–1729
Sawamura Kodenji as Tsuyu no Mae, 1698
Hand-colored woodblock print
20⅞ × 12⅛ in. (53 × 30.8 cm)
Signature: Wagako Torii Shobei
Seal: Kiyonobu
Publisher: Hangiya hammoto; date: 1698,
third month
John Chandler Bancroft Collection, 1901.59

This is one of the many rare Japanese prints in the Museum's renowned John Chandler Bancroft Collection. It is the only complete impression of the first single-sheet print by Kiyonobu, the founder of the Torii school, which specialized in depictions of the Kabuki theater. Kiyonobu arrived in Edo (modern Tokyo) from Osaka in 1687 with his Kabuki-actor father and began to issue books, prints, and Kabuki signboards in the 1690s. As pictures of real actors in performance were introduced by Kiyonobu, such prints became a Torii school trademark.

This large sheet depicts the star *onnagata* (male actor of female roles) in the play *Kanto Koroku.* In the role of Tsuyu no Mae, the actor is performing a *kyoran* (lunatic dance) before the Tadasu Shrine. The fluid contours and rounded forms echo the movements of the elegant *wagoto* (soft-stuff) style of Kyoto-Osaka (Kansai) Kabuki, which Kiyonobu knew through his father.　　　—EdeSS

MIYAGAWA CHOSHUN

Japanese, 1682–1752
*Pictures of Amusements at
Cherry-Blossom-Viewing Time*
Kyōhō period (1716–36)
Pair of six-panel folding screens; ink, color,
and gold on paper
(a) 45½ × 117½ in. (115.5 × 298 cm)
(b) 45⅜ × 116⅟₁₆ in. (115.9 × 294.8 cm)
Signature: Nihon e Miyagawa Choshun zu
(on each screen)
Seal: Unidentified (left screen only)
Harriet B. Bancroft Fund and Stoddard
Acquisition Fund, 1993.72.1–2

The preeminent painter of the first half of the
eighteenth century, Miyagawa Choshun was
the founder of the mainstream of *ukiyo-e*
painting, or pictures of the floating world.
Known for his hanging scrolls of beautiful
women and handscrolls of seasonal genre
scenes, he did not design woodblock prints
or illustrated books as did most artists of this
school. Only one other pair of screens, in a
Japanese collection, is attributed to him.

These rare screens are marvels of execution. All the figures interact convincingly to

create a sense of relaxed merriment. The right screen depicts a cherry-blossom-viewing party at an elegant Edo teahouse. Men and women enjoy activities both indoors and out: drinking sake, playing the samisen, and strolling beside the pond. The left screen represents boating on Edo's Sumida River. The famous Ryogoku Bridge, the center of the most important Edo amusement area, is shown on the far right. In the individualization and variety of characters crossing the bridge and walking along the riverbank, these exquisite screens reflect the influence of Hishikawa Morunobu (died 1694), whom Choshun acknowledged as his stylistic source. The delicacy and elegance of line and color reveal Choshun's personal style. No detail is treated summarily; attention is paid to describing the patterns of textiles, the decoration on lacquer and porcelains, and the materials and construction of architecture.

—EdeSS

KAIGETSUDO DOSHIN

Japanese, active 1700–16
Courtesan
Hanging scroll; ink and opaque color
on paper
43⅞ × 19⅝ in. (111.4 × 49.7 cm)
Signature: Nippon giga Kaigetsu matsuyo
Doshin zu (a pleasure picture in Japanese
style drawn by Doshin, a last leaf of
Kaigetsu)
Seal: Ando
John Chandler Bancroft Collection,
1901.1345

The gorgeously attired and worldly woman of the licensed pleasure quarter is the basic motif of *ukiyo-e,* a distinct style of painting, book illustration, and prints that arose from and gave visual identity to the new urban culture of the Edo period (1600–1868). Doshin's painting depicts the classic type; identified by neither name nor house, this standing figure of a high-class courtesan represents an ideal of feminine beauty devoid of dramatic or narrative interest. The painter's signature and seal declare his adherence to the style of his contemporary Kaigetsudo Ando, who lived in the Asakusa district of Edo and specialized in paintings with rich color and powerful contour lines. Decorative designs on the outer and under kimono reveal an interest in fashion shared by both the painter and his public. The evening-glory (*yugao*) pattern shown against a woven fence recalls for readers of Japanese literature the poignant romantic emotions associated with the fourth chapter of the classic novel *The Tale of Genji.*

—EdeSS

NAGASAWA ROSETSU

Japanese, 1754–99
Bamboo, 1790s
Six-panel folding screen; ink on paper
50¾ × 102³⁄₁₆ in. (128.9 × 261.1 cm)
No signature
Seals: (upper) Nagasawa, (lower) Gyo
Eliza S. Paine Fund, 1970.4

Better known for bizarre figure paintings with strong color and eccentric brushwork, Rosetsu demonstrated his breadth in the present painting, a relatively peaceful work. It is characterized by broad brushstrokes, interrupted only by the nodes of the bamboo, and by a dependence on ink tone rather than line in defining form. The date can be inferred from the condition of the lower seal, known to have been broken at its upper right corner in 1792.

At about age twenty-five Rosetsu became the pupil of the Kyoto painter Maruyama Okyo, one of the most popular and prolific Japanese artists of the eighteenth century. Within four years he had become a respected painter in the Okyo tradition of detailed linear description of objects, his work differing from that of his master in its greater dynamism in composition and distortion of line. In 1786–87, after a trip to the southern part of Kii Province, the younger artist turned away from a linear style to one based on washes and shading.   —EᴅᴇSS

YOSA BUSON
Japanese, 1716–83
Travelers on Horseback on a Mountain in Spring, 1770s
Four-panel folding screen; ink, light colors, and gold on paper
67⅛ × 105⅞ in. (170.5 × 268.9 cm)
Signature: Shunseisha
Seals: (upper) Shachoko,
(lower) Sha Shunsei
Eliza S. Paine Fund, 1961.7

In contrast to most Japanese painting schools of the Edo period (1600–1868), Nanga artists including Buson looked for inspiration to Chinese scholar painting—the work of cultivated amateurs—that they knew through woodblock-printed books. The woodblock medium changed the intentionally bland brushwork of the Chinese style into a stronger two-dimensional design, creating simplified surface patterns and flat ink tones that appealed to Japanese taste.

Buson used a Chinese theme for this work, but instead of imitating a specific prototype, he followed the Japanese idea of selecting a style appropriate to his subject. The asymmetrical composition recalls the type created by the professional painters of the Southern Song (1127–1271) and Ming (1368–1644) periods, whose work formed the foundation of Japanese ink-painting styles. *Travelers on Horseback* may be one of a set of four screens depicting the seasons—a major theme in Japanese painting. Buson was also one of Japan's best haiku poets, and the lyrical style of this painting reveals qualities found in his poetry: momentary impressions characterized in simplified evocative images.   —EDESS

SAKAI HOITSU

Japanese, 1761–1828
Cranes
Two-panel folding screen; ink, colors, and
gold on paper
56½ × 56⅜ in. (143.5 × 143.3 cm)
Signature: Hoitsu Kishin hitsu
Seals: (upper) Oson, (lower) Monsen
Charlotte E. W. Buffington Fund, 1964.9

In their arrangement of two-dimensional
forms on the picture surface and dramatic use
of a gold ground, Hoitsu and his pupils are
truly heirs to the great tradition of Japanese
decorative painting. Born in Edo (modern
Tokyo) into a wealthy samurai family, Hoitsu
experimented with a variety of idioms before
finally taking up the Rimpa style of Ogata
Korin (1658–1716). He was responsible for a
Rimpa revival in nineteenth-century Edo, and
he published two woodblock-printed books
on Korin, including the *Korin hyakuzu* (One
hundred paintings of Korin) in 1815. This
two-panel screen is virtually a "quotation"
from a pair by Korin at the Freer Gallery
of Art in Washington, D.C. Hoitsu's version,
however, is less naturalistic than the painting
on which it is based.   —EdeSS

YOKOI KINKOKU

Japanese, 1761–1832
Landscape, after 1810
Six-panel folding screen; ink and light
color on paper
67 × 136 in. (170.2 × 345.4 cm)
Signature: Kinkoku
Seal: Kinkoku
Alexander H. Bullock Fund, 1986.2

A lover of nature and a follower of the
mountain-climbing Shugendo sect, Kinkoku
sought to express the vitality and flux inher-
ent in the physical world. His association
with haiku poets during his years in Nagoya
(1795–1823) inspired an interest in and admiration for the Nanga painter Yosa Buson.
After studying Buson's mature landscapes,
Kinkoku's early painting style—based on the
more naturalistic Maruyama-Shijo school—
was transformed.

The spontaneity and individualism implicit in Nanga ideals are evident in this "Chinese" landscape of towering mountain peaks
and huts around a lake. More dynamic than
Buson's work, Kinkoku's painting shows the
use of washes to create tone, loose strokes to
depict mountain forms, and a variety of freely
applied brushwork to suggest foliage. Dots
scattered over the picture surface unify the
composition visually.   —EdeSS

Bowl with Attached Pedestal
>5th century A.D. or earlier
>Korean, Paekche or Kaya
>Unglazed gray stoneware with deposits
>of accidental ash glaze
>H: 9⅝ in. (24.5 cm) DIAM: 14¾ in. (37.4 cm)
>Alexander H. Bullock Fund, 1988.143

In Korea, as in the other countries of northeastern Asia, ceramics have long been an important form of artistic activity; pottery shards carbon dated to the beginning of the ninth millennium B.C. have been found there. Notwithstanding their debt to developments in China and their profound influence on Japanese ceramics, Koreans produced ceramic wares that are fundamentally different from those of their neighbors. Transforming Chinese prototypes, they introduced new shapes, decorative devices, and technical innovations. One of the most revolutionary changes occurred in the first century B.C. with the appearance of a hard gray pottery made with the potter's wheel. Unglazed stoneware in powerful shapes, imaginatively decorated and fired at a higher temperature, developed during the following centuries. Discovered in graves and the foundations of palaces and other buildings, these ceramics are associated with the upper classes.

This wide-mouth bowl with pedestal is of the type related to early Chinese pottery and bronze shapes. Hand built by the coil method and finished on the wheel, its body was fired to stoneware hardness and burnished a dark gray color where not covered by streaks, splotches, and natural ash glaze. A convex band and triangular perforations enliven the pedestal.   —EDESS

Shakyamuni Buddha
>   late 1st–early 2nd century A.D.
>   Indian (Katra Mountains, Uttar Pradesh)
>   Mottled red sandstone
>   H: 20¹¹⁄₁₆ in. (52.5 cm) W: 23⅝ in. (60 cm)
>   D: 7¼ in. (18 cm)
>   Alexander H. Bullock Fund, 1985.240

The image of Shakyamuni—the historical personage called the Buddha, or Enlightened One, who lived in India in the sixth century B.C.—made its first appearance in art in the late first century A.D. This fragment of a well-known Buddha image—characterized by a coiled topknot on the head—was produced early in the reign of Kanishka, the third ruler of the Kushan dynasty, and belongs to the type created in the Mathura region of North India. Typical attributes of Buddha figures in this period are a monastic robe, long ears, a cranial bump, a round mark between the eyes, a halo, and the right hand raised in the gesture of reassurance. Carved in relief on the slab behind the deity's right arm are leaves of the Tree of Wisdom (*bodhi*), under which the historical Buddha attained enlightenment. This figure of Shakyamuni, originally seated cross-legged in the lotus position, radiates a spirituality and repose that is entirely appropriate to the Buddha. The soft, tactile surfaces of the flesh and the warm, mottled sandstone create a sensuous and compelling image.

—EDESS

Standing Shakyamuni Buddha
>3rd century A.D.
>Northwest Indian (Gandhara)
>Gray schist with traces of gesso
>H: 50⅝ in. (148.9 cm) W: 20½ in. (52 cm)
>D: 11½ in. (29.2 cm)
>Museum purchase, 1926.2

Two different artistic centers produced early images of the Buddha: Mathura, in the Indian heartland, and Gandhara (now in Pakistan), in the northwest. This standing Buddha from Gandhara, a border area of the Roman Empire, is related stylistically to the late Roman figures of the empire's Asian outposts. Its iconography, however, is Indian, and the image has the customary attributes of a Buddha figure of this period—monastic robe, cranial bump, topknot of hair, dot on the forehead, and long ears. The right arm, broken off, probably made the sign of reassurance; the left hand holds the robe in a typical gesture. The scene on the base depicts Shakyamuni, the historical Buddha, preaching, with two disciples on either side.

As in many Gandharan Buddhas, the style is a mixture of formulas. While deeply cut drapery falls convincingly over the body, revealing the form beneath, the rigid frontality of the pose works against the naturalism of the slight swaying of the hips and the bent right knee. The figure was originally polychromed or gilded and attached to the wall of a Buddhist building. —EdeSS

Brahma
> 10th century A.D.
> South Indian (Tamil Nadu), Chola dynasty
> Granite with traces of gesso and red pigment
> H: 50⅜ in. (148.4 cm) W: 29⅜ in. (74.5 cm)
> D: 18⅝ in. (47.3 cm)
> Eliza S. Paine Fund, 1964.16

Shiva, Vishnu, and Brahma are the major gods of Hinduism, and their functions are often interchangeable. An ancient god whose authority was derived from the Vedas (the scriptures of the ancient Aryans), Brahma retained his importance as the creator in Hinduism, although no cult comparable in size to those of Vishnu and Shiva developed around him.

Broad, powerful shoulders, elegant proportions, and the exquisite workmanship of the jewelry identify this sculpture as a tenth-century Chola work. Looking at the four directions, the four faces of Brahma symbolize the four Vedas as well as the cardinal points of the compass. Two of the image's four original arms are now lost. The missing upper hand probably made the gesture of reassurance, while the lower one held a lotus. The upper left hand holds and counts a rosary; the lower left, now empty, may have held a pot containing the water from which the universe was created. Because the sculpture is not meant to be viewed in the round, the back of the figure is more shallowly carved and lacks the precise modeling of the front.   —EdeSS

Somaskandamurti
11th–12th century
South Indian, Chola dynasty
Bronze
H: 19⅛ in. (48.6 cm) W: 23½ in. (59.7 cm)
D: 11⅜ in. (28.9 cm)
Museum purchase, 1951.93

The full lips, prominent noses, and smooth volumes of these figures characterize the art of the Chola dynasty, whose Shivaite rulers controlled South India from the tenth to the twelfth century—a period when bronze casting flourished. Somaskandamurti is a manifestation of Shiva, the greatest god of the Hindu trinity, seated on Mount Kailasa, the mountain throne of the gods. The multiple aspects of Shiva are combined in three personages: the god himself, his consort Parvati, and his son Skanda. This type of representation is peculiar to South India, where it originated during the Pallava period (about fifth to ninth century).

Depicted sitting with one leg bent in the position of royal ease, Shiva holds an ax (symbol of his power) and an antelope (symbol of his rule over the beasts of the wilderness). His lower hands make the gestures of holding a flower and of assurance. Parvati sits in a mirror image of her consort's pose, wearing a cord with a marriage symbol around her neck. Her gestures symbolize granting a gift and holding a flower. An atypical feature is the projecting section of the base on which their son Skanda, the demon slayer, is placed. Usually he appears standing or sitting alongside his parents on a rectangular block.

—EdeSS

Parvati, Consort of Shiva
    12th–13th century
    South Indian, Chola dynasty
    Bronze
    H: 19¹¹⁄₁₆ in. (50 cm) W: 7⁹⁄₁₆ in. (19.2 cm)
    D: 6⅞ in. (17.5 cm)
    Museum purchase, 1928.26

In the first half of the Chola period bronze casters created some of the greatest masterpieces of Indian art. The grace and beauty of this icon, whose pose recalls the movements of the dance, is a part of that tradition. Unlike Indian stone sculpture, which was often part of an architectural setting, bronze images like the one shown here are complete in themselves. Carried in procession, they were covered with clothing, jewels, and flower garlands, which hid the sensuous form that is the embodiment of the South Indian ideal of beauty. This posture, the crown of matted locks (*jatamukuta*), and the sacred cord that passes between her breasts are attributes of Parvati (Daughter of the Mountain). She is consort to Shiva, one of the three primary Hindu gods, and she functions as his *sakti* (female energy), embodying the active principle and strength of the deity. Parvati also represents the benevolent aspect of the Great Mother, the ancient Indian fertility goddess.

—EDeSS

A Lady and a Gentleman Converse, from the *Tuti-Nama*
about 1580
Indian, Mughal dynasty
Opaque watercolor on paper, heightened with gold; mounted on a later album page
6⅜ × 3¾ in. (17 × 9.5 cm)
Persian text in *nastaliq* script; chapter heading in *kufic* script
Islamic Rug Deaccessioning Fund, 1991.33

The *Tuti-Nama* (Tales of a parrot) is a collection of fifty-two fables compiled by the Persian writer Ziya'ud-din Nakshabi in the fourteenth century. In this popular work the parrot recounts diverting tales to his mistress in order to prevent her from being unfaithful to her absent husband. The tales must have been a favorite of the Mughal emperor Akbar, as two lavishly illustrated copies were produced during his reign. The page shown here once belonged to the second of these manuscripts (housed in the Chester Beatty Library in Dublin), which is incomplete in its present state. It is difficult to link the picture with a particular tale, because it lacks specific identifying details. The *nastaliq* passage below the painting, from the story of three farmer brothers (the forty-ninth night in the series), has been transposed and does not relate to the image. Likewise, the illuminated heading, a later addition, does not belong to the manuscript.

In its simple, symmetrical composition and restrained movement, this work reflects the influence of the great painters of the Persian Safavid court. It is Indian in mood and feeling, however, recalling northern pre-Mughal painting in its warmer palette, larger figures, and true profile of the facial contours. Akbar's interest in the visual world is evident in the shading that gives greater realism to the hard outline of the figures.   —EDeSS

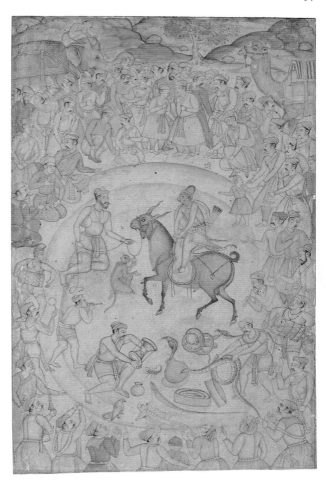

*Performers and Animals at an Impromptu
Circus in the Countryside*
>about 1590
>Indian, Mughal dynasty
>Drawing in brush, washes, and color
>on paper
>Persian *nastaliq* calligraphy on verso
>attributed to Mir Ali
>15¾ × 8½ in. (40 × 21.6 cm)
>Islamic Rug Deaccessioning Fund, 1989.110

Fine drawings of this type were popular during the last decades of the reign of Akbar, the greatest of the Mughal emperors. They were often included with paintings in illustrated manuscripts of the period or were mounted in albums containing paintings and alternating pages of calligraphy. The borders of the present drawing, once part of an imperial album, were trimmed and the original format was altered when the album was dispersed.

The disparate elements of this scene, whose meaning is unclear, are blended masterfully in a circular composition. It illustrates an impromptu performance of five musicians and three animal handlers before a crowd of fifty-three eager men and boys. The amusements include animal combats orchestrated by a man with an hourglass and, at the center, a circus act with two monkeys and a strange hybrid creature. The presence of this beast, with the combined features of a donkey and a goat, suggests that the subject is not a genre scene but rather the illustration of a legend or fable.

—EDESS

A Ruler on Horseback Leading an Army across a Battlefield, from the *Tarikh-i Alfi*
about 1592–94
Indian, Mughal dynasty
Opaque watercolor on paper, heightened with gold
Persian text in *nastaliq* script
15¾ × 8½ in. (40 × 21.6 cm)
Alexander H. Bullock Fund, 1985.315

Unlike the painting of the Hindu Rajput courts, Mughal painting incorporated Persian, Western, and Indian elements. The *Tarikh-i Alfi* (The History of one thousand years)—the first of many lavish illuminated manuscripts commissioned by the Mughal emperor Akbar—was to be a new history of the Muslim world with information dating from the death of Muhammad to Akbar's day. Today only fragments of this famous manuscript survive, perhaps twenty-six from about three hundred illustrated pages. They are distinguished by the large size of the folios, the occasional inclusion of several scenes on the same page, and the relationship of images to text. The ruler depicted here, leading an army across a battlefield, was probably Al-Hasan ibn Sahl, governor for the Abbasid caliph Al-Mamun (reigned A.D. 813–33). A landscape with the distant view of a village appears along the top, and there is a notation on the lower margin naming Sur Das Gujarati, one of the most accomplished artists in Akbar's imperial atelier, as the painter of the miniature. (A second notation is illegible.)

—EdeSS

Ewer and Basin
    18th century
    Indian (Deccan)
    Bidri ware (cast metal alloy of zinc, copper,
    and lead with silver inlay)
    Ewer H: 12¼ in. (31 cm) W: 13⁹⁄₁₆ in.
    (34.5 cm) D: 7¼ in. (18.5 cm)
    Basin H: 7¼ in. (18.4 cm)
    DIAM: 14⅞ in. (38.8 cm)
    Islamic Rug Deaccessioning Fund,
    1989.163.1–3

The arts that flourished in the independent kingdoms of the Deccan derived their inspiration not only from the Mughal empire—North India, Persia, and West Asia—but from local traditions as well. Among such objects that display originality in both design and technique is bidri ware, whose earliest craftsmen were probably Persians patronized by the ruler of the Deccan in the fifteenth century. As the descendants of the original Persian artisans became Indian, local Muslims and some Hindus joined the bidri industry. Composed of a uniquely Indian metal alloy inlaid with silver and then coated to create a permanent black surface, bidri ware was made in a great variety of shapes and sizes, including trays, cups, *huqqa* (water-pipe) bases, ewers, and wash basins.

The superb craftsmanship and luxuriant floral designs of this ewer and basin suggest that they were made for someone of high station. Their shape, material, and decoration transform humble utilitarian objects into outstanding examples of courtly taste.

—EdeSS

Candlestick
    mid- to late 13th century
    Anatolia (eastern Turkey)
    Bronze, engraved and inlaid with gold
    and silver
    H: 8 in. (20.9 cm) DIAM: 7½ in. (19.4 cm)
    Museum purchase, 1949.16

Metalwork has long been a prestigious art form in West Asia, evoking the highest technical and artistic virtuosity from the makers of both secular and religious objects. In the twelfth century Muslim metalworkers in eastern Persia decorated their bronze vessels with engraved animal figures and vegetal ornament and inlaid them with precious metals. Spreading westward during the next century, the inlay technique was used with great skill and imagination in the workshops of Egypt, Iraq, Syria, and eastern Turkey.

The decoration of this candlestick—which includes revelers, musicians, polo players, and falconers—is typical of much Islamic metalwork, as are the good wishes written in ornamental script. On the object's neck is an inscription invoking "long life, auspicious fate, good fortune, and godliness"; on its body is writing that proclaims "divine favor" and "spiritual integrity" in addition to wishes of good fortune.   —EdeSS

Bahram Gur Hunting the Wild Ass, from the *Great Mongol Shahnama of Firdausi*
about 1335–36
Persian (Tabriz), Ilkhanid dynasty
Opaque watercolor on paper
23⅝ × 15¹³⁄₁₆ in. (60 × 40.5 cm)
Jerome Wheelock Fund, 1935.24

Bahram Gur, whose name means "wild ass," was a Sassanian king (reigned A.D. 430–38) renowned by legend for his hunting prowess. Having performed a miraculously difficult shot, he acknowledged the divine aid involved in his skill by ordering six hundred wild asses branded with his name and six hundred marked with gold earrings and distributed to the people.

The painting shown here is one of fifty-eight remaining miniatures from an early illustrated example of the Persian national epic; this particular manuscript is known as the "Demotte" Shahnama after the art dealer Georges Demotte, who separated and sold the folios individually. The work is believed to have been commissioned by Ghiyath-al-Din, a high official (*vizir*) at the Ilkhanid court at Tabriz. Its large and sumptuous pages illustrate the introduction to Persian painting of conventions, especially in landscape depiction, derived from Chinese art. Providing the cultural links for such artistic influence were the Mongol conquests of Asia and Europe in the thirteenth century and their control of China, Central Asia, and Persia.   —EdeSS

Kai Khusraw Giving His Testament, from the *Shahnama of Firdausi*

> 1494
> Persian (Gilan)
> Opaque watercolor on paper
> 13⅜ × 9⁹⁄₁₆ in. (34.6 × 24.2 cm)
> Calligraphy in *nastaliq* script with chapter heading in *naskh*
> Jerome Wheelock Fund, 1935.23

Kai Khusraw Giving His Testament was removed from a volume of the Persian national epic, the *Shahnama,* executed for Sultan Mirza Ali, ruler of Gilan. This enormous manuscript once contained about 350 miniatures, which are now dispersed. Rendered in one of the manuscript's two distinct painting styles, the Worcester page exemplifies the "big-headed" type, named after its most singular characteristic. Although no artists' names are recorded, the scribe is Salik ibn Said. The literal translation of the title given in the text over the painting is "Kai Khusraw appointing Gudarz-e Keshvad executor and distributing properties and possessions."

The *Shahnama* relates that Shah Kai Khusraw sank into depression after defeating all his enemies and was told by an angel in a dream to depart this world. Despite the pleas of his courtiers, he dictated his last wishes and vanished in a snowstorm. Here the depressed ruler is shown surrounded by seven warriors.

—EdeSS

The Prophet Zakariya in the Tree,
from a *Falnama*
> about 1550
> Persian (Tabriz or Qasvin), Safavid dynasty
> Opaque watercolor on paper
> 23⅜ × 17⅝ in. (58.4 × 44.8 cm)
> Calligraphy on reverse in *nastaliq* script
> Jerome Wheelock Fund, 1935.16

This painting is one of twenty-nine known pages from a dispersed manuscript of the *Falnama* (Book of divination), which has been dated to the reign of Shah Tahmasp and attributed to Aqa Mirak and Abd al-Aziz, artists at his court. The manuscript was extraordinarily large. Its paintings depict episodes from the lives of the Old Testament prophets, Jesus, and Muhammad and his family, as well as scenes of heaven and hell. No text appears on the paintings, but inscriptions on the back of each include poetic references to the prophets and forecast the future of the person who is using the book. In this case the writing on the reverse refers to the *miraj,* or night ascent of the prophet Muhammad, and lists divinations said to derive from commentaries of the Greek physician Galen. A depiction of the *miraj* (now in the Arthur M. Sackler Gallery, Washington, D.C.) faced this text.

Illustrated here is the story of the prophet Zakariya (a conflation of Zacharias, the father of John the Baptist, and the Old Testament prophet Zachariah), who according to Muslim legend died a martyr's death. Escaping his pursuers by hiding in a tree that miraculously opened to admit him, Zakariya was betrayed by Iblis, the devil, who pointed out the hem of the prophet's cloak protruding from the trunk. The devil's forces sawed the tree apart and with it Zakariya, whose saintly aura is shown as flames bursting among the leaves.

—EdeSS

Attributed to SHAYKH MUHAMMAD
Persian, active second half of 16th century
Weeping Man Drying His Eyes,
third quarter of 16th century
Ink drawing on paper
4 ¹¹⁄₁₆ × 2 ⅛ in. (11.9 × 5.3 cm)
Signature of Bihzad and date 892 (1486)
added later
Museum purchase, 1935.17

Too large to be a preliminary sketch for a manuscript painting, this superb drawing is a moving example of the single-figure studies that became popular at the sixteenth-century Safavid court. It is attributable to Shaykh Muhammad, who was responsible for paintings in some of the best royal manuscripts of that time, as well as many independent single-page works. The hallmarks of his style in the present drawing include the spiraling turban folds and "viscerally" bunched sleeve drapery of the weeper's robe.

Shaykh Muhammad's tenure in the Safavid royal atelier came after the death of the older painter Bihzad, whose name was inscribed here for profit or prestige at a later date. The signature of Bihzad, the most famous Persian miniature painter, is found on many works postdating his career of the late fifteenth and early sixteenth century.

—EdeSS

Bayezid I, "The Thunderbolt," Routs the Crusaders at the Battle of Nicopolis, from the *Hunernama of Loqman*

> 1584
> Turkish (Istanbul), Ottoman dynasty
> Opaque watercolor and ink on paper
> 18⁹/₁₆ × 11³/₁₆ in. (47.2 × 28.5 cm)
> single page
> Jerome Wheelock Fund, 1935.13

This painting is from the largest and one of the finest illustrated works containing historical paintings from the Ottoman classical period. The manuscript, minus three—including this one—of its original forty-five illustrations, is now in the Topkapi Saray Museum in Istanbul. It was completed by the court historian Loqman and copied by the calligrapher Sinan ibn Mehmed the Bosnian. Documentary evidence links the Ottoman court painter Osman and several other famous artists to the work. Individual paintings have not, however, been attributed to specific artists.

The Turkish text of this folio is taken from an account of the rule of Ottoman Sultan Bayezid I (reigned 1389–1403). In 1396 Venetian and Hungarian crusaders besieged the Bulgarian fortress of Nicopolis, which was held by the Ottomans. Although Bayezid I was at that time attempting to take Constantinople from the Byzantines, he abandoned his campaign to hurry to Nicopolis, where he inflicted a crushing defeat upon his Christian rivals. He appears as the mounted swordsman with the large, multiplumed turban in the center of this painting. The image appears on the left side of a double folio; its related text follows on both sides of the adjoining page.

—EdESS

Flowering Plant beside a Pond
first half of 17th century
Persian, Safavid dynasty
Silk: cut, voided satin velvet, brocaded
45 ⁷⁄₁₆ × 26 ¾ in. (115.4 × 68 cm)
Jerome Wheelock Fund, 1938.2

A great patron with wide-ranging interests, Shah Abbas (reigned 1586–1628) is best known for his architectural transformation of Isfahan. Already the richest city in the empire, Isfahan became a major artistic and cultural center under Abbas's patronage. Because he was interested in developing arts that were important for trade, the shah established workshops throughout Persia to produce textiles, rugs, and ceramics. From these state-supported industries came luxury objects that were essential economic assets to compete with Chinese and other foreign goods in the domestic and the export markets.

The elegant taste of Shah Abbas's textile workshops is evident in the use of precious materials—silver and gold—and complex weaving techniques. Patterning this silk fragment is a large flowering plant growing out of a tiny "pond" in schematic wavelike form. Rhythmic and fluid in their combined effect, the individual units create an undulating surface design of subtlety and grace.   —EdeSS

Ancient Art

Statuette of a Man
   about 3000–2500 B.C.
   Mesopotamian (Sumer), dynastic period
   Limestone and shell
   H: 13 3⁄16 in. (33.5 cm) W: 4¾ in. (12 cm)
   D: 4¾ in. (12 cm)
   Museum purchase, 1937.91

In the early third millennium B.C. the Sumerians lived in independent city-states on the vast, fertile plains of Mesopotamia between the Tigris and Euphrates rivers. The focal point of their settlements was the temple—the god's earthly residence and the city's economic center.

Found beneath the floor of a temple at Khafaje, northeast of Baghdad, this imposing statuette of a bearded man stands in a posture of austere piety. His carefully patterned beard and fringed skirt identify him as either a high priest or a god. The figure is highly stylized with little reflection of musculature or naturalistic proportions, the head expressing devotion and power through the exaggeration of facial features. Enlarged, staring eyes made of shell inlaid in bitumen project a concentrated intensity, which is accentuated by crescent-shaped brows. Squared arms and tightly clasped hands add to the figure's strength.

—SHA

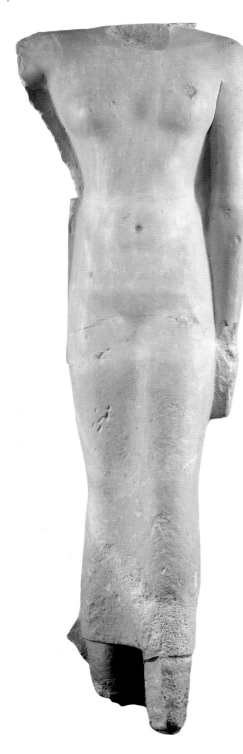

The Royal Descendant Hetepheres
 about 2440 B.C.
 Egyptian, early Fifth Dynasty
 Limestone
 H: 54⅛ in. (137.4 cm) W: 17½ in. (44.6 cm)
 D: 10⅜ in. (26.5 cm)
 Museum purchase, 1934.48

Hetepheres was the mother of the pharaoh's hairdresser, Re-Wer, who was honored in a stone tomb at Giza. Carved in high relief from a single slab, this life-size statue of Hetepheres was originally part of a family sculptural group of five figures that included her husband, son, and grandchildren. Her sculpted likeness furnished a recognizable image for her *ka,* or life essence, to inhabit, should her mummified physical body be destroyed. It also served as a focal point for veneration by her survivors, who would visit the necropolis on feast days.

   Now headless, Hetepheres stands with her left arm at her side; her right arm was once raised, probably to embrace a grandchild. Enlivened by the subtle modeling of swelling breasts, slender waist, and hips revealed beneath a sheer garment, the rigid, artificial pose of the figure—fixed for eternity—is typical of Old Kingdom art.   —SHA

Ay, Fan Bearer
about 1360 B.C.
Egyptian, Eighteenth Dynasty
Plaster on limestone with polychrome
H: 13 9⁄16 in. (34.5 cm) W: 8 13⁄16 in. (22.3 cm)
D: 2 1⁄8 in. (5.3 cm)
Austin S. and Sarah C. Garver Funds,
1949.42

Ay was a favored courtier of the pharaoh Akhnaten and vizier under his successor Tutankhamun. Here Ay is depicted as a powerful royal advisor, holding the fan, crook, and scarf that symbolize his fidelity to the king. His flesh is colored a reddish brown, typical of males in Egyptian art.

Succeeding Tutankhamun, who died prematurely, by marrying the boy king's widow,

Ankhesenamun, his own granddaughter, Ay died after a brief rule of four or five years. This fragment, carved in sunken relief, comes from a wall in his tomb at Tell el Amarna on the eastern bank of the Nile. In its entirety the relief showed him kneeling in worship with his family and surrounded by a long prayer inscribed in hieroglyphics. The style of Ay's portrait is typical of the Amarna period in its naturalistic depiction of the narrow and bony face, long nose, and small, squinty eyes—features common to other surviving representations of him.   —SHA

A Winged Genius
>   883–859 B.C.
>   Assyrian (Nimrud)
>   Alabaster
>   93 ¼ × 52 ½ in. (236.7 × 133.4 cm)
>   Museum purchase, 1930.42

The Assyrian kings, who ruled in Mesopotamia from the ninth through the seventh century B.C., projected an image of themselves as all-powerful, divinely sanctioned monarchs. They adorned their palaces with monumental friezes that displayed their authority and wealth.

This low relief, once painted in bright colors, belonged to a series of slabs adorning the fabulous palace of the great ruler Assurnasirpal II at ancient Kalhu (biblical Calah, or modern Nimrud), the Assyrian capital in central Iraq. Standing in profile, according to artistic convention, the figure in the frieze is a winged "genius," or protective being. He wears the horned cap, knee-length tunic, and long, fringed cape associated with divinities. Whether fertilizing the Tree of Life or anointing the king (depicted on another slab), the genius clutches in his raised right hand a conical date-palm spathe, the male part of the flower. In his left hand he holds a small pail that would have contained a magical liquid or pollen. Running through the chiseled relief like an incantation is a cuneiform inscription detailing the king's ancestry and achievements such as his prowess in warfare and hunting and his march to the Mediterranean in search of cedar timbers for his palace.

—SHA

Figure of a Warrior
> late 6th century B.C.
> Greek
> Bronze
> H: 5⅝ in. (14.3 cm) W: 2½ in. (6.4 cm)
> D: 1¾ in. (4.5 cm)
> Museum purchase, 1936.45

Ancient warriors often dedicated diminutive bronze figurines at sanctuaries in southern Greece as symbols of gratitude for good fortune in battle. This solid-cast hoplite, or infantryman, whose compact form, severe lines, and iconography are characteristic of Lakonian (Spartan) workshops of the late sixth century B.C., was allegedly found at Sparta. The attacking pose is typical of a soldier striding forward with his right arm raised. The spear and shield he once carried are now lost. His close-fitting cuirass, or breastplate, is incised with spirals that echo the forms beneath, and his short chiton, gathered up about the hips (perhaps for a running charge), bears lightly incised ornamental crosses. To protect his shins the warrior is equipped with greaves. A Corinthian-style helmet exposes the figure's beard, while his hair is worn long and falling over his shoulders in typical Spartan fashion.   —SHA

Attributed to the RYCROFT PAINTER
    Greek (Attica)
    Amphora, about 530–520 B.C.
    Slip decorated earthenware with
    incised details
    H: 24½ in. (62.3 cm) DIAM: 14⅜ in. (37.3 cm)
    Austin S. and Sarah C. Garver Funds,
    1956.83

Greek vase painters often depicted narratives
by showing a chosen moment from an episode
of great importance to a story or myth. These
favorite episodes became formulaic representations of myths, some serving as parables
for contemporary events. The figures could
be identified by the attributes, symbols, or
objects that surrounded them.

    The work of the so-called Rycroft Painter,
first identified in the Rycroft Collection in
England, is characterized by extremely fine
draftsmanship, especially in the rendering
of equine anatomy. Chariot scenes and depictions of the wine god Dionysos were among
his favorite subjects. One side of this beauti-
fully preserved black-figured vase shows Her-
mes, the messenger god, squiring Leto, mother
of the twin deities Apollo and Artemis, to the
august company of the Olympian gods. Leto
appears mounting a chariot with her adult
children. On the other side Dionysos wears
a crown of vine leaves and raises his drinking
cup. He is flanked by dancing maenads who
play *krotala* (similar to castanets) and by lust-
ful satyrs. Since the amphora was frequently
used as a container for wine, the imagery of
Dionysos is particularly appropriate.

—SHA

Head of a Female Votive Figure
early 5th century B.C.
Greek (Cyprus)
Limestone
H: 20 in. (50.8 cm) W: 13¾ in. (34.9 cm)
D: 16¼ in. (41.3 cm)
Museum purchase, 1941.49

This monumental head, originally painted, belonged to an over-life-size statue of a votive figure or deity from Cyprus. While its exact function is unknown, the statue probably stood in a sanctuary. The amalgam of styles evident here reflects the tumultuous history of Cyprus during the first millennium B.C.: this eastern Mediterranean island was ruled by Assyria and Egypt in quick succession, and in the mid-sixth century, it developed strong ties with eastern Greece while both were part of the Persian Empire.

The sensitively modeled oval face with almond eyes, high cheekbones, and smile indicates an affinity with art from eastern Greece in the Archaic period. On the headdress a throng of maenads and silens, companions of the Greek wine god Dionysos, dances through a colonnade topped with rosettes. Whereas column capitals in the form of heads of the goddess Hathor (just below the rosettes) reveal artistic kinships with Egypt, the feathered brows and the treatment of elaborately curled and patterned tresses suggest Assyrian influence.   —SHA

ERETRIA PAINTER
  Greek (Attica)
  Pyxis, about 430 B.C.
  Slip decorated earthenware
  H: 4 ½ in. (11.4 cm) DIAM: 5 ½ in. (14 cm)
  Museum purchase, 1935.148

During much of the age of the great states-man Perikles (the later fifth century B.C.), Athens was embroiled in a long and bitter civil war. Weary of fighting, Athenians increasingly rejected the depictions of battle scenes on pottery in favor of peaceful motifs of heavenly gardens with young, playful divinities. Most popular was Aphrodite, goddess of love and beauty and the antithesis of war. Very common at this time were pyxides, small containers for perfume and cosmetics, whose use might transform the average Athenian housewife into the love goddess herself.

On the lid of this pyxis are depicted two pairs of playful Erotes, the companions of Aphrodite. One pair holds roosters in preparation for a fight, while the other displays a leashed rabbit (symbol of erotic love) to a potential lover. Around the cylindrical body are three vignettes of an aristocratic woman at leisure in her home with a maidservant in attendance. The so-called Eretria Painter was an accomplished artist whose interest centered on charming, intimate scenes, displaying the fashions and pastimes of the rich. These portrayals, replete with intriguing details of costume, hairstyle, and furnishings, represent an idealized stereotype of daily life for Athenian upper-class women who lived isolated at home.   —SHA

Grave Stele: Old Man
> late 4th century B.C.
> Greek (Athens)
> Pentelic marble
> H: 73¾ in. (187.5 cm) W: 24¾ in. (63 cm)
> D: 15¼ in. (39 cm)
> Museum purchase, 1932.2

This over-life-size figure exemplifies the elaborate relief sculpture that marked graves in Athenian cemeteries from the third quarter of the fifth century until the late fourth century B.C. Such funerary sculptures were typically set within a rectangular architectural frame with side pilasters supporting a cornice and pediment. They usually showed the deceased accompanied by a member of the family, a slave, or a prized possession. Often two figures are present, one standing and one seated, the latter probably representing the dead individual.

In the present example, a fragment of a larger stele, an old man leans heavily on his staff while gazing downward, presumably at the deceased (now missing). Carved almost in the round, the full figure is rendered naturalistically with a sagging breast and veined hands indicative of old age. Hollow, deep-set eyes and a furrowed brow express the pathos of loss and quiet longing characteristic of fourth-century style.   —SHA

Cinerary Urn
>mid-2nd century B.C.
>Etruscan (Vignagrande)
>Terra cotta with traces of polychrome
>H: 44¼ in. (112.4 cm) W: 35⅛ in. (89.3 cm)
>D: 20¾ in. (52.7 cm)
>Museum purchase, 1926.19

This urn, found in a tomb near Chiusi in central Italy, reveals the mastery of the Etruscan craftsman in molding terra cotta. Modeled in high relief and in the round, the work conveys emotional pathos and drama. Once painted, it still bears traces of red, blue, vermilion, brown, and yellow.

The figure of the old man on the top portrays the deceased, whose ashes were contained within the urn. Propped up on pillows, he reclines as if enjoying a banquet in a conventional pose that was later copied by the Romans. Characteristic of Etruscan portraiture is the unflinching naturalism of the wrinkled face and flabby body—specific features that would have identified the man to friends and family. The six figures engaged in vigorous combat on the front panel of the base suggest that the deceased was a soldier. On the ends, under the arched entrances to Hades, wait the dread figures of Vanth, goddess of the dead, and Charun, escort of the dead. The latter, winged and wearing a lion skin, owns the hammer that rests on the altar beside him.   —SHA

*Prince Arikankharer Slaying
His Enemies*
>   A.D. 25–41
>   Meroitic
>   Sandstone
>   H: 8⁷⁄₁₆ in. (21.4 cm) W: 10 in. (25.4 cm)
>   D: 1⅞ in. (4.9 cm)
>   Museum purchase, 1922.145

Contemporary with early imperial Rome, the Meroitic civilization flourished along the fertile banks of the Nile River in the land of Kush in what is now the Sudan. This African dynasty traded not only with Egypt to the north but also with Greece, Rome, and peoples of the Near East. Consequently, official Meroitic art reflects the absorption of external influences adapted to serve local rulers.

Arikankharer belonged to the black royal house of Kush, whose capital was at Meröe. Although the crown prince died before he could come to power, this superbly carved, raised relief shows him as a vigorous, victorious conqueror. Behind him floats a female Winged Victory, brushing away flies, while between his legs a vicious dog mutilates a fallen enemy. As the prince's father, King Natakamani, imported sculptors from Egypt, the work is hybrid in nature. Distinctly Meroitic in style and detail are the compact proportions, round head, curly hair, oversize eyes, flabby neck, and broad shoulders of the prince as well as the portrayal of fear in the faces of the vanquished. The imperial stride, the smiting pose, and the convention of showing the figure partially in profile are attributes assimilated from Egyptian art.   —SHA

*The Drinking Contest of Dionysos
and Heracles*
     about A.D. 100
     Roman (Antioch)
     Mosaic
     72 3/16 × 73 5/16 in. (183.4 × 186.2 cm)
     Museum purchase, 1933.36

Throughout much of the 1930s, the Worcester
Art Museum joined four other institutions in
excavating Antioch, one of the four great cities
of the late Roman Empire. First a mobilization
point for Roman military campaigns against
the Parthians, it had prospered under Julius
Caesar and Augustus and grown into a cultural and political center, flourishing until
an earthquake devastated the city in A.D. 526.
Among the greatest treasures unearthed at
Antioch were numerous mosaics from public
and private buildings.

This pavement, reflecting the realistic
space of late Hellenistic painting, was one of
five that decorated the floor of a triclinium,
or dining room, of an elegant villa from the
first Roman period of the city. Fittingly, it
depicts a mythical symposium, or drinking
contest, with Dionysos, the god of wine,
reclining at the center. Crowned with vine
leaves in his luxuriant curls, the pale god
displays the empty cup that he has drunk
dry. A ruddy Heracles is on his knees, chal-
lenging Dionysos. Silenus, on one side, and
Ampelus (a child personifying the vine), on
the other, give the victory to the god, while
a slave girl at the left plays the double flute.

—SHA

Portrait of a Lady
    A.D. 138–192
    Roman
    Bronze
    H: 21¼ in. (54 cm) W: 18½ in. (46.9 cm)
    D: 13⅜ in. (34 cm)
    Sarah C. Garver Fund, 1966.67

During imperial times upper-class Roman women had far more freedom than did their counterparts in classical Athens. They were able to participate in society, dine with their husbands, and attend parties, games, and shows as well as political gatherings. This rare, life-size portrait bust may have come from a large family shrine of an emperor, perhaps Marcus Aurelius or Septimus Severus. Found together but not attached as a single unit, the head and shoulders, which were probably paired in antiquity, each reflect a different quality of workmanship. While the bust and shoulders are treated summarily, the head is sensitively modeled and the hair minutely detailed in carefully combed waves. The woman's heavy-lidded gaze betrays a contemplative personality as distant as the emperors themselves.　　—SHA

Head of a Man
(possibly *Diocletian*)
      A.D. 300–10
      Roman
      Black basalt
      H: 8 in. (20.3 cm) W: 6⅜ in. (16.3 cm)
      D: 6¹³⁄₁₆ in. (16.7 cm)
      Alexander H. Bullock Fund, 1974.297

During the reign of the Tetrarchs (A.D. 284–312), rule over the Roman Empire was divided among four men, each responsible for different regions. Most of their surviving portraits are carved in porphyry, a hard, dark stone that is difficult to work. The resulting sculptures were often blocklike in style, far removed from physical likeness.

This portrait is thought to represent Diocletian, one of the Tetrarchs, who ruled the region from Thrace to Egypt for more than twenty years before he abdicated in A.D. 305. Carved in basalt, a material similar to porphyry, the forceful, cubic head shows features characteristic of the emperor: furrowed brow and expressive, enlarged eyes conveying tension and concern. The downward curve of the mouth suggests a tough and resolute man whose advancing age is apparent in his sunken cheeks and receding hairline.   —SHA

Hunting Scene
early 6th century A.D.
Late Roman (Daphne)
Mosaic
20 ft. 6¾ in. × 23 ft. 9¾ in. (6.26 × 7.16 m)
Museum purchase, 1936.30

This pavement, excavated from a villa at
Daphne, a resort in the hills above ancient
Antioch, depicts the hunting of dangerous
game, an aristocratic pastime represented
in mosaics and other media throughout the
Roman world and commonly at Antioch. At
the center stands a hunter ringed by animals
in a pattern much like that of an oriental car-
pet. Hunters on foot and horseback attack a
variety of animals with sword, spear, and bow
and arrow, a weapon used by Parthians and
Persians to the east.

Situated near the eastern coast of the
Mediterranean Sea, the great city of Antioch
became a confluence for cultural influences
from western Greco–Roman traditions as
well as eastern Persian sources. While the
dress style in this work is that of Hellenistic
Greece, the ornamental use of nature and the
figures' stiff poses derive from the art of ancient Parthia (now northern Iran). The animals, portrayed more naturalistically than
the human figures, are used to fill compositional voids in a decorative fashion, resulting
in the flat, two-dimensional creation characteristic of Antioch at this time.   —SHA

European Art

Capital

> early 12th century
> French (Bourges)
> Limestone
> H: 27 in. (68.8 cm) W: 24 3/4 in. (62.8 cm)
> D: 24 3/4 in. (62.8 cm)
> Museum purchase, 1941.42

This capital, once part of a column in the nave arcade of Notre-Dame de Montermoyen (now destroyed), is a clear statement of the revival of monumental stone carving after almost seven centuries of neglect. Inspired in part by the vestiges of acanthus-leaf capitals of Roman architecture, the medieval carver has replaced the classical leaf forms with monstrous animals and humans like those that appear in twelfth-century books and wall paintings. On the lower range of the capital are facing lions, each munching a leg of a pathetically naked man who is also being seized from above. A monster setting its teeth into the man's skull displays its double body on two sides, submitting to the strict geometry of the capital's shape. As the monster ultimately dissolves into a serpent's tail, it becomes entwined with the tail of a similar beast so that the ghoulish feast continues without a break on all four corners of the block. While to a twentieth-century eye the monsters may seem threatening, the renowned twelfth-century cleric Saint Bernard of Clairvaux betrayed a certain admiration for such imagery of "fierce lions . . . a four-footed beast with a serpent's tail . . . many bodies under one head . . . marvelous and deformed comeliness (and) comely deformity."

—VCR

Chapter House

> 1150–60 and 1180–90
> French (Le Bas-Nueil)
> Limestone
> H: 14 ft. 8½ in. (4.48 m) W: 32 ft. 8 in.
> (9.96 m) D: 21 ft. 9 in. (6.62 m)
> Museum purchase, 1927.46

This rare example of medieval architecture, originally from the Benedictine Priory of Saint John at Le Bas-Nueil in west-central France, once served the needs of a small celibate community of men engaged in a life of prayer, study, and reflection. The room was part of a self-contained monastic complex consisting of church, sleeping quarters, storage areas, common dining area, cloister walk, meeting rooms, and prior's (or director's) quarters. In the chapter house consisting of one room, the religious community would gather daily to discuss its business affairs and assign the duties of the members.

Common to French and Spanish regions, this twelfth-century architecture characterized by stone vaulted ceilings was the first development in western Europe to rival the sophistication of the Roman world. The ceiling is divided into six compartments of quadripartite vaults springing from piers in the four corners of the room and supported in the center by two monolithic columns. The visually dynamic division of the ceiling is echoed in the rounded forms of the windows and their columnar supports.   —VCR

Episode from *The Legend of the Seven Sleepers of Ephesus*

> about 1205
> French (Rouen)
> Stained glass
> 24 15/16 × 23 5/16 in. (63.3 × 59.2 cm)
> Museum purchase, 1921.60

This panel of stained glass, dating from the age of the great French cathedrals, was originally one of thirty-six scenes in a tall Gothic window from Rouen Cathedral. The entire window was dedicated to an account of the miraculous resurrection of seven Christian martyrs after centuries of sleep—a tale that confounded those who doubted the belief in the resurrection of the body. This episode shows two messengers coming to announce the news of the miracle to the Byzantine emperor Theodosius II.

The narrative is relayed by conventions common to medieval storytelling: the building represented by a single arch, exterior and interior spaces differentiated by red and blue backgrounds, and the drama of the meeting suggested primarily through gesture. Highly colored sections of glass in blue, red, yellow, violet, and green were cut to fit the figural design; and details of faces, garments, and architecture were drawn on the glass with dark brown vitreous washes. After the drawn details were fired onto the surface, the segments of glass were joined together with lead cames (grooved bars) and set within a complex iron framework. The entire structure was enclosed in one of the great stone window openings of the cathedral's nave.

—VCR

*The Crucifixion with the Virgin
and Saint John*

> late 13th century
> Spanish (Oviedo, Asturias)
> Wood with polychrome
> Christ H: 67 3/8 in. (171 cm) W: 12 7/8 in.
> (32 cm) D: 10 3/4 in. (27.2 cm)
> Virgin H: 59 1/8 in. (150.1 cm) W: 13 1/4 in.
> (33.6 cm) D: 8 1/4 in. (20.9 cm)
> Saint John H: 61 1/8 in. (155.2 cm) W: 14 in.
> (35.4 cm) D: 8 in. (20.2 cm)
> Museum purchase, 1934.26a, b, c

Becoming popular in Christian devotion around the ninth century, the image of the crucified Christ was commonly depicted during the next four centuries as alive and often crowned, thus evoking both his human suffering and the eternal triumph of his conquest of death. In the thirteenth century, however, Christ's agony and the sufferings of those who witnessed his death began to be emphasized. This group is remarkable because of its impressive size and its survival as an ensemble, including two witnesses, the disciple John and the Virgin Mary. The deity once wore a royal crown (an attribute still retained by Mary), in accordance with traditional depictions of Christ's divinity and rulership.

Once brightly colored with paint, this wood sculpture reflects a transition in style from the thirteenth to the fourteenth century; the rhythmic curves of the exposed ribs, the terraced drapery, and the stiffness of John and Mary continue the more abstract rendering of earlier medieval art, while the soft, oval faces of all three figures and Christ's sagging body and downcast head convey the emotional appeal of an emerging style.   —VCR

Virgin and Child

about 1300
French (Paris)
Ivory with traces of gilding and polychrome
H: 8 3/8 in. (21.3 cm) W: 3 3/16 in. (8.1 cm)
D: 15/16 in. (2.3 cm)
Museum purchase, 1940.27

By the fourteenth century the great age of
cathedral building was over. Patrons and donors shifted their interest from large public
monuments to the commissioning of private
devotional objects. The sophisticated carving
and rare materials of this small ivory suggest
that it was destined for personal veneration
by a patron of high social standing. Reflecting
artistic skill of the highest level, the feminine
grace and courtly elegance of the Virgin and
Child are underscored by the sway of the figure and the liquid movements of the garment
folds. Traces of gilding and color can be seen
in the border of the Virgin's robe. To possess
an object of this quality validated the privi-
leged social status of the owner.   —VCR

*The Last Supper and the Agony
in the Garden*

about 1300
Italian (Spoleto)
Fresco transferred to canvas
92 5/8 × 100 15/16 in. (235.4 × 256.3 cm)
Museum purchase, 1924.24

In the Italian medieval and Renaissance periods episodes of sacred history and dogma were often depicted in fresco on expanses of wall instead of on windows of stained glass, the preferred medium for large works of art in northern Europe. Fresco was carried out by applying a thin coat of wet plaster to a section of the wall and executing the design progressively on each newly surfaced area. Rich earth tones of color penetrated the surface of the wet plaster and bonded with the wall.

In this fresco from the Church of Santa Maria inter Angelos near Spoleto, two different episodes of Christ's life, the Last Supper and the Agony in the Garden, are combined within a single frame, a juxtaposition typical of medieval concepts of narrative. These subjects were popular choices for the walls of monastic refectories (dining halls) as well as churches. Also typical of its time is the spatial rendering, which seems inconsistent and awkward to the modern viewer: the tabletop is seen at an angle, but the dishes are depicted in profile view. The apostles surrounding Christ, who sits at the apex of their triangular configuration, are gathered improbably on one side of the table. The decorative folds of the tablecloth, the jeweled halos, and even the linear highlights of the garments emphasize decorative patterning of the surface rather than the illusionistic space and three-dimensional form that were to become artistic features of the centuries following.

—VCR

MASTER OF THE FOGG PIETÀ

Italian, 14th century
Saint Francis, about 1350
Painting on panel
38 1/8 × 14 5/8 in. (96.9 × 37.2 cm)
Museum purchase, 1923.19

The Master of the Fogg Pietà, to whom this work is attributed, is so named after a small painting by the same hand at the Fogg Art Museum at Harvard University. The distinctive style has enabled art historians to attribute a number of works to that artist, even though virtually nothing is known of his life and identity. It is believed that he worked in Florence and was greatly influenced by the rich, decorative surface of paintings produced in nearby Siena. The Master of the Fogg Pietà continued a tradition begun by the early Renaissance painter Giotto, in which the modeling of the figure, in this case Saint Francis, helps to create a more realistic depiction of form and space.

Saint Francis, who founded the religious order of the Franciscans in the early thirteenth century, is represented here over one hundred years later. He is easily recognized by the stigmata, marks corresponding to the wounds that appear on Christ's hands, feet, and side. The inscription on the scroll records part of the Epistle of his Mass. In addition to *Saint Francis,* the Worcester Art Museum owns a twin panel depicting Saint Philip; both panels appear to have been part of a large altarpiece.

—JAW

Attributed to STEFANO DA VERONA

> Italian, 1375–after 1438
> *The Virgin and Child with Angels in a*
> *Garden with a Rose Hedge,* about 1430
> Painting on panel
> 23 $^{15}/_{16}$ × 17 in. (60.8 × 43.2 cm)
> Museum purchase, 1912.63

This painting has long been attributed to Stefano da Verona, who was active mostly in northern Italy and who was a proponent of the International Style. Popular throughout Europe toward the end of the fourteenth century, this style embodies a decorative elegance and an interest in minute detail that derive from northern European painting. Here the Virgin is portrayed as the Madonna of Humility: instead of being enthroned, she is seated on a cushion on the ground. In the sky above her appear God the Father with a scepter and the Holy Spirit in the form of a dove. The rose garden symbolizes the purity of the Virgin, while the music-making angels evoke the refined and grace-filled court life of the very end of the Middle Ages.   —JAW

PESELLINO

Italian, about 1422–57
A Miracle of Saint Silvester, 1450s(?)
Oil on panel
12 3/16 × 30 7/8 in. (31 × 78.5 cm)
Museum purchase, 1916.12

Pesellino, the Renaissance artist whose given name was Francesco di Stefano, was influenced by his fellow Florentine painter Fra Filippo Lippi. He painted mainly small panels, usually richly colored and carefully executed. This work, along with two others (now in the Doria Pamphili collection in Rome), once formed the lower portion of a large altarpiece. (Known as a predella, this section generally consists of narrative scenes that elaborate on the altarpiece's main theme.) The three panels illustrate episodes in the life of Saint Silvester, who was pope from 314 to 335 during the reign of Constantine the Great. In the Worcester painting Silvester is seen kneeling in prayer before a bull, which he miraculously restores to life in a contest with a magician. By his action Silvester convinces Constantine, who sits at the far left, and his mother, Helen, seated at the extreme right, that they were correct in converting to Christianity. The entire scene takes place in a Renaissance-style loggia, or arcaded gallery.   —JAW

Madonna and Child
second half of 15th century
German (Cologne) or Flemish
Bronze
H: 26 ³/₄ in. (68 cm) W: 9 ¹¹/₁₆ in. (24.6 cm)
D: 9 in. (22.9 cm)
Museum purchase, 1951.33

Most of the sculpture made in Germany and the Netherlands during the fifteenth century was carved from wood, which makes this bronze piece quite rare. The production of such a large bronze required a complicated casting process in which the figure was first modeled in clay. Probably designed for an altar or niche and intended to be viewed frontally, the Madonna has a groove at the back of her head that is likely to have held a crown. That the figures reveal no attempt at idealization, either in the description of the faces or in the overall proportioning, is characteristic of northern European art from the late middle ages. Shown in a rather awkward pose and with somewhat homely features, the Christ Child in particular reflects a shift in this period toward a more humanistic depiction of sacred subjects.   —JAW

Ceiling from a Domestic Room
second half of 15th century
Spanish
Wood with polychrome
23 ft. × 19 ft. 5 in. (7 × 5.92 m)
Museum purchase, 1952.18

This elaborate ceiling, one of the rare examples surviving from its time, demonstrates the importance of domestic architecture at the end of the middle ages. By the late fifteenth century wealthy merchants as well as the landed nobility would have had the resources to commission a room with such a ceiling. All surfaces are richly embellished with paint, the curving leaf forms in deep greens against a warm red background. Within defined rectangles, the lush, naturalistic foliage forms rhythmic motifs similar to those found in textiles and in the decorative margins of contemporary manuscripts. The lavishness of the surface pattern lightens the visual effect of the massive structural design of the ceiling. Four master beams under narrow transverse supports ride on brackets at the juncture of the walls. Heraldic badges, common forms of identifying family lineage, appear on end panels between the beams.   —VCR

LORENZO DI CREDI
 Italian, 1459–1537
 A Miracle of Saint Donato of Arezzo,
 about 1479–85
 Painting on panel
 6½ × 13³⁄₁₆ in. (16.6 × 33.5 cm)
 Theodore T. and Mary G. Ellis Collection,
 1940.29

Toward the end of the fifteenth century,
Lorenzo di Credi began his career in Florence, which had become the leading center
of painting in Italy. Among those working
with Lorenzo in the workshop of the Florentine artist Verrocchio was Leonardo da Vinci,
who also influenced him.

This panel once formed part of a predella,
or lower portion of an altarpiece, made for the
cathedral of Pistoia in central Italy. The subject
of the Worcester panel is Saint Donato, who
proved the innocence of a tax collector falsely
accused of theft. The saint is shown assisting
the man in locating the money that his deceased wife had hidden for safekeeping. Saint
Donato appears also in the main panel of the
Pistoia altarpiece, which was commissioned
in memory of Bishop Donato de' Medici.

—JAW

SCHOOL OF PROVENCE

French, late 15th century
The Christ of Saint Gregory,
about 1480–90
Painting on panel
30½ × 38⅜ in. (77.4 × 97.5 cm)
Museum purchase, 1938.80

Probably designed originally as an altarpiece, this painting represents the mystical vision of Gregory the Great when, according to legend, Christ appeared to the saint as he celebrated the Mass. As it is the actual vision that is represented, the saint is not included. The resurrected Christ sits at the edge of the tomb supported by two angels and bearing the marks of his suffering and death on the cross: a lance wound in his side, nail holes in his hands, and a crown of thorns piercing his brow as well as marks left by the scourging that preceded his crucifixion. Such realistic representations were popular during the late middle ages as the result of widespread cults devoted to the wounds and blood of Christ. The rich gold textile seen behind the Messiah includes pomegranates in its design as a symbol of eternal life. While the work appears to have been painted in the southeastern part of France, the realistic imagery may well have been inspired by examples from northern France.

—JAW

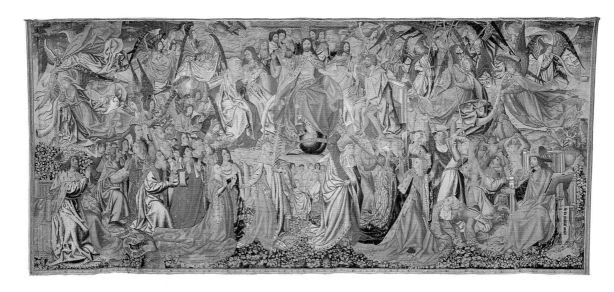

The Last Judgment
    about 1500
    Flemish
    Wool tapestry
    12 ft. 6 in. × 26 ft. 6 in. (3.81 × 8.08 m)
    Museum purchase, 1935.2

Tapestries were a popular form of wall covering in the late middle ages, not only as decoration but also for the protection they provided from the damp, cold stone walls of buildings. By about 1400 tapestry weaving had reached a high degree of craftsmanship. This large work was probably woven in Brussels, which dominated the tapestry-manufacturing industry in Europe from the mid-fifteenth century through the end of the seventeenth. Over one hundred almost life-size figures make up a complex representation of the Last Judgment. Seated at the center is Christ in Majesty, who separates the blessed on the left from the damned on the right. The artist who designed the work may well have been Hugo van der Goes (1440?–82), one of the leading Flemish painters of the time.   —JAW

PIERO DI COSIMO
Italian, 1462–1521
The Discovery of Honey by Bacchus,
about 1499
Painting on panel
31 ³⁄₁₆ × 50 ⅝ in. (79.2 × 128.5 cm)
Museum purchase, 1937.76

Piero di Cosimo, who painted a number of important religious pictures, was a rather mysterious artist; his eccentric personality was reflected especially in his paintings of strange animals and fantastic scenes. In this allegorical setting the mythological figures of Bacchus and Ariadne, in the right foreground, are accompanied by satyrs and maenads who make noise to attract a swarm of bees to settle in a hollow tree. The result is the discovery of honey, considered a step forward in the history of civilization which is symbolized in the background by the juxtaposition of an idyllic view of a town (on the left) and a wild and forbidding landscape (on the right).

This painting resulted from the private patronage that developed in fifteenth-century Italy. Representative of a new demand for secular subjects, *The Discovery of Honey by Bacchus* is one of a pair of panels commissioned for the home of Giovanni Vespucci of Florence. The other, now in the Fogg Art Museum at Harvard University, is titled *The Misfortunes of Silenus.*   —JAW

QUENTIN MASSYS
Flemish, 1466–1530
The Rest on the Flight into Egypt,
about 1509–13
Oil on panel
32⁹⁄₁₆ × 31⅛ in. (82.6 × 79 cm)
Museum purchase, 1937.4

Massys was the leading master of his time in Antwerp. International in his outlook, he combined the carefully detailed and brilliantly colored surfaces of the Flemish tradition with the more monumental and expressive figure types found in Italian and German art. *The Rest on the Flight into Egypt* was originally part of an ensemble of eight paintings representing the Seven Sorrows of the Virgin, made for the main altar of a monastery near Lisbon. The other panels are also now in museums, seven in Lisbon and one in Rio de Janeiro. In the Worcester panel, against a scene of slaughter taking place in the background, the Holy Family is shown resting during their flight to Egypt to escape King Herod's execution of all children in Bethlehem two years and younger. Massys's sensitive rendering of the expressive faces of the main figures conveys the deep emotions associated with this event. His attention to the landscape, in particular the complex rock formations, is notably advanced for the period.   —JAW

ALBRECHT DÜRER
   German, 1471–1528
   Coat of Arms with a Skull, 1503
   Engraving on cream laid paper
   8⅝ × 6³⁄₁₆ in. (21.9 × 15.7 cm) sheet
   Sarah C. Garver Fund, 1966.36

Dürer was the most important northern European printmaker of the Renaissance. He was a virtuoso engraver and woodcut designer who also experimented with etching. One of a handful of artists, authors, and scholars who brought the Renaissance from Italy to the North, he went twice to study the classicizing and scientific secrets of the Italian masters. Dürer was among the first artists to study anatomy and to utilize theories of ideal human proportions, and his style is precise and naturalistic.

This image is a *memento mori,* a reminder of the brevity of life and mortality. From medieval times, the skull was universally understood as a symbol of death. The woman is costumed in an elegant Nuremberg party dress and the sort of crown worn by a bride at her wedding. Her partner is a wild man, one of a mythical savage race believed to live in the impenetrable forests of the Alps. He symbolizes lust, the opposite of the spiritual ardor embodied in chivalry. Thus, the mismatched couple stands for sacred and profane love, both of which are inevitably conquered by death.

—DA

GIULIO CAMPAGNOLA
Italian, about 1482–1515/16
Saint John the Baptist, about 1505
Engraving on cream laid paper
11⁹⁄₁₆ × 9⁷⁄₁₆ in. (29.4 × 24 cm) sheet
Bequest of Mrs. Kingsmill Marrs, 1926.1442

John the Baptist, a forerunner of Christ, was considered by theologians as the last of the Old Testament prophets and the first saint of the New Testament. A contemporary of Christ's, he preached the coming of the Messiah. Here he is identified by the baptismal cup that he holds. This print, made in northern Italy, is remarkable for the physically palpable form and dimension of the figure, combined with an evocation of atmosphere. To suggest the misty effects of light, the artist stippled the copper plate with his graver, rather than incising lines.

A versatile gentleman scholar of the Renaissance, Campagnola was a painter, engraver, poet, musician, scholar, and typographer. Born the son of a writer in Padua, he worked at the ducal court at Ferrara, and by 1509 he was in Venice. There he fell under the influence of the painter Giorgione, whose evocative, atmospheric painting style inspired Campagnola to make his most revolutionary prints.   —DA

Donor Portrait of Prior Peter Blommeveen
      1510–30
      German (Cologne)
      Stained glass
      27 ½ × 22 ½ in. (68 × 56.5 cm)
      Museum purchase, 1920.105

By the fifteenth century northern European stained-glass designers as well as painters and sculptors demonstrated an increasing ability to represent the tangible nature of the real world. In this fragment of a window from the Monastery of Saint Barbara in Cologne, the figure, located in a believable three-dimensional setting, is depicted with the accuracy of a portrait likeness. The prior Peter Blommeveen, the donor of the window, is portrayed with a shield bearing a crosier and two "blossoming" branches that provide a visual pun on his surname.

The German Renaissance artist who made this panel retained earlier techniques of assembling colored glass set in a lead matrix, but his segments—larger than those of his predecessors—include more white glass. He also used the new method of silver-nitrate stain to achieve the various shades of yellow visible in the architecture. The full-bodied modeling of the figure and the richly worked crosier and damask robe (cope) recall images from the north nave windows of the Cathedral of Cologne, executed by the workshop of Hermann Pentelinck after designs of the contemporary panel painter known as the Master of Saint Severin.   —VCR

ANDREA DEL SARTO
Italian, 1486–1530
Saint John the Baptist, about 1517
Oil on panel transferred to canvas
28 × 19¾ in. (71.1 × 50.2 cm)
Museum purchase, restricted funds; gifts
from Louise I. Doyle, Britta D. Jeppson,
The Reverend and Mrs. DeWolf Perry in
memory of Harriett Brooks Hawkins, the
Worcester Art Museum Members' Council,
and anonymous donors, 1984.38

One of the leading painters in Florence during the early sixteenth century, Sarto produced this representation of Saint John the Baptist, the patron saint of Florence, at the height of his artistic career. The graceful design and blending of rich colors reflect the idealized style of the High Renaissance, as does the artist's combination of Christian and classical traditions. The Baptist appears with his usual attributes, a coarse hair shirt and a pointing hand, which here directs attention to a simple reed cross symbolizing Christ. The wreath in the saint's hair alludes to Bacchus, who was considered during the Renaissance to be a pagan prototype of Christ. Similarly, Saint John, the last of the Old Testament prophets, prepared the way for Christ and, like Bacchus, lived in the wild.

One of only a handful of paintings by Sarto in America, *Saint John the Baptist* was brought to this country in the mid-nineteenth century and was for the most part unappreciated until it was rediscovered in 1977 in a church in Worcester.   —JAW

PARMIGIANINO (GIROLAMO FRANCESCO MARIA MAZZOLA)

Italian, 1503–40
Three Old Men, about 1535
Red chalk drawing on cream laid paper
6¼ × 5⅞ in. (15.8 × 14.9 cm) sheet
Museum purchase, 1951.49

The most influential master of Italian Mannerism, Parmigianino developed a personal style that was widely imitated throughout Europe in the following generations. He was a remarkable draftsman, and hundreds of his drawings survive. Some relate specifically to his paintings and prints, while many others reflect the activity of a compulsive, continually inspired artist. This seemingly quick and unplanned sketch represents three emaciated old men, perhaps ascetic monks or philosophers, who resemble the mysterious sage standing in the background of Parmigianino's famous painting *The Madonna of the Long Neck* (now in the Uffizi Gallery in Florence). It is assumed that the drawing dates from the same period, when the master worked in Parma around 1535. The craggy bodies and scowling expressions of these old men in their tattered garments imply a disregard for the outside world. Their wizened faces and contemplative expressions suggest the wisdom of age and experience. Although the poses seem doddering, there is an elegance in the figures' artificially attenuated, gnarled limbs.

—DA

SCHOOL OF FONTAINEBLEAU
French, about 1550–70
Woman at Her Toilette
Oil on panel
44 × 34½ in. (111.7 × 87.6 cm)
Museum purchase, 1932.23

Fontainebleau, the famous French royal residence, was the site of great artistic activity in the mid-sixteenth century during the rule of Francis I. Developed at this court and nearly unique to it was the concept of a boudoir portrait, depicting the sitter in intimate circumstances. The Worcester panel has been connected specifically with François Clouet (about 1510–72), who served as court painter at Fontainebleau under both Francis I and Charles IV. Clouet was greatly influenced by Italian Mannerist portraiture with its emphasis on refined elegance and a great clarity and precision of draftsmanship.

The subject of this work—identified variously as Diane de Poitiers, Mary, Queen of Scots, and other figures of royalty—remains unconfirmed. Several variants of this composition exist, supporting the theory that a famous prototype must have been their common inspiration.   —JAW

EL GRECO (DOMÉNIKOS THEOTOKÓPOULOS)

Spanish (born in Crete), 1541–1614
The Repentant Magdalen, about 1577
Oil on canvas
42½ × 39⅞ in. (107.9 × 101.4 cm)
Museum purchase, 1922.5

El Greco (the Greek) is considered one of the greatest of inspired visionary artists. A native of Crete, he first worked in Italy before settling in Toledo, Spain, where he had a successful career with major commissions from both the Church and the private sector. *The Repentant Magdalen* bears the artist's signature in Greek and is believed to have been painted around 1577, shortly after El Greco's arrival in Spain. The elongation of the figure and the dramatic sky, hallmarks of his style, were to become even more pronounced in his later work. Saint Mary Magdalen was a favorite subject of El Greco's and one he returned to again and again. Here she is depicted as a repentant prostitute living the life of a hermit, her contemplation of eternal life after death symbolized by her dramatic, upward glance and by the skull at the lower left. Standing next to the skull is the Magdalen's most common attribute: the vase of ointment with which she annointed Christ's feet. —JAW

HENDRIK GOLTZIUS
Dutch, 1558–1617
Hercules and Cacus, 1588
Chiaroscuro woodcut on cream laid paper
16⅛ × 13 1/16 in. (41 × 33.2 cm) image
Bequest of Mrs. Kingsmill Marrs, 1926.182

This image shows one of the many exploits of Hercules, the most famous hero of ancient mythology, who vanquished supernatural foes with his great strength and courage. On one occasion, driving his herd through Latium, the region where Rome would one day be established, Hercules stopped to nap on the bank of the Tiber River. While he slept, Cacus, a fire-breathing monster who terrorized the countryside, stole the cattle, dragging them backward by their tails into his cave. When the hero awoke he followed the animals' lowing to the demon's lair, where he killed Cacus.

A prolific draftsman and painter and an engraver of unmatched virtuosity, Goltzius was the most successful printmaker of the Mannerist period in the Netherlands. He designed the chiaroscuro woodcuts produced in his shop in Haarlem, which were probably made by other craftsmen in his employ. Using several carved blocks of wood to print different tones of color, the artist simulated the effect of a pen drawing heightened with wash.

—DA

FRANCESCO VANNI
Italian, 1563–1610
Saint Ansano Baptizing the Sienese,
about 1593
Black and red chalk drawing on cream
laid paper
16¹¹⁄₁₆ × 10¹⁵⁄₁₆ in. (42.3 × 27.7 cm) sheet
Museum purchase, 1951.54

A prominent painter in the Tuscan city of
Siena at the beginning of the seventeenth
century, Vanni executed several major altar-
pieces for the churches of his hometown.
This drawing was made in preparation for
an altarpiece for the Cathedral of Siena, a
painting commissioned in 1593. Varying in
some details from the final painting, which
still stands in the cathedral, the study is quite
finished in appearance. Its style and technique
mark Vanni as a follower of Federico Barocci,
a master from Urbino, who became famous
for his work for the powerful Medici family
in Florence, and for the pope in Rome.

The legendary Ansano, who was born into
a noble family in Siena in the fourth century,
became an influential preacher of the Christian faith at the age of twelve. His father was
loyal to the Roman emperor Diocletian, and
after trying unsuccessfully to control his re-
bellious son, he condemned Ansano to death
when the saint was just twenty years old. The
altarpiece represents Ansano as a pious youth
baptizing the converted Christians. Christ is
gloriously enthroned in heaven above, while
the Virgin Mary intercedes for the Sienese.

—DA

ADRIAEN VAN DE VENNE
Dutch, 1589–1662
*Winter Landscape with Skaters
near a Castle,* 1615
Oil on panel
6½ × 9⅛ in. (16.4 × 23.2 cm)
Charlotte E. W. Buffington Fund, 1951.30

Van de Venne was a poet and a versatile artist whose work ranged from extremely colorful paintings of historical and allegorical subjects to monochromatic illustrations of proverbs. He painted this small winter scene early in his career while living in Middelburg, one of the major trading centers of the new Dutch republic. The bird's-eye view and intense coloring recall the Flemish landscape tradition of the sixteenth century, which had been established by artists like Pieter Brueghel the Elder. A variety of anecdotal figures represent all levels of Dutch society, from the worker chopping wood at the lower left to the well-dressed patricians enjoying the outdoor activities of winter. This painting is one of a set of four landscapes by van de Venne that make up the Four Seasons, a popular theme in northern European art. (The two representing spring and summer are at the J. Paul Getty Museum in Malibu, and the one depicting autumn is in a private collection.)　　　　　—JAW

JACQUES BELLANGE
French, 1594–1638
The Annunciation, about 1616
Etching and engraving on cream laid paper
13⅛ × 12¹⁄₁₆ in. (34 × 32.2 cm) sheet
Bequest of Mrs. Kingsmill Marrs, 1926.686

At a time when Italian painters and sculptors were working in the dramatic, naturalistic idiom that we call Baroque, a small group of artists in France revived the elegant, self-conscious style of Mannerism. One of these masters was Jacques Bellange, a painter, decorator, and printmaker who worked as a court artist at Nancy, capital of the independent duchy of Lorraine. The artist's position at court is attested by his knighthood, which he proudly noted when signing his prints.

Bellange's work combines aristocratic refinement with elements of religious mysticism. This etching represents the moment when the Virgin Mary, interrupted at her weaving with a prayer book open beside her, learns from the Archangel Gabriel of the impending birth of Christ. As she looks up at God's messenger, who presents her with a lily, the symbol of purity, her face reflects innocence and piety—simple emotions that contrast with the artificiality of the image. The artist's religious fervor is expressed in the intensity of this glance, as well as in the archangel's silhouetted profile and the balletic hand gestures. The proportions of the figures are unnaturally attenuated, and their postures are constricted and twisted. They are pressed close to the picture surface, while the background is a confusing array of furniture, draperies, clouds, and flashing rays of light.

—DA

PIETER LASTMAN
Dutch, 1583–1633
Paris and Oenone, 1619
Oil on panel
19¼ × 28⅛ in. (48.9 × 71.4 cm)
Gift of Mr. and Mrs. John Adam, Jr., 1984.39

One of the leading painters of religious and mythological subjects at the beginning of Holland's Golden Age, Lastman is also recognized as the principal teacher of Rembrandt. He is the most accomplished of a group of artists often called the "pre-Rembrandtists," who were skilled at portraying narrative scenes. Their goal was to illustrate stories in a straightforward fashion, often using expressive gestures and naturalistic elements.

Lastman painted at least three versions of this subject, which comes from an ancient Greek legend. Paris, who had been raised by shepherds, makes love to the nymph Oenone, who in turn bestows on him a floral wreath, signifying her consent to giving up her virginity. The young couple is surrounded by elements relating to the theme of love. The dog and the embracing figures at the left symbolize fidelity, while the goats, melon, and bagpipes on the right all represent sexual activity. The right-hand elements forecast the fate of this young couple, whose marriage ended when Paris deserted Oenone for Helen of Troy.

—JAW

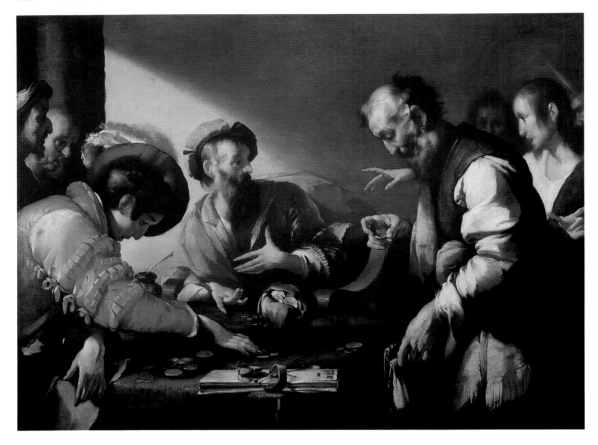

BERNARDO STROZZI
Italian, 1581–1644
The Calling of Saint Matthew,
about 1620
Oil on canvas
54¾ × 73⅝ in. (139.1 × 187 cm)
Museum purchase, 1941.1

Strozzi, a Capuchin monk, was one of the greatest early seventeenth-century Italian painters. His works are often marked by strong contrasts of light and dark, which became one of the hallmarks of Italian Baroque painting. Taken from the Gospel of Saint Matthew, this scene shows Christ asking Matthew, a tax collector, to join him as one of his disciples. Christ appears at the far right, barely identified by the hint of a halo at the back of his head. The strongest light falls on Matthew, who appears awestruck, while his assistants go about their business of counting money. The restlessness in the figure of Matthew is echoed throughout the painting by the animated brushwork and dramatic positioning, including a variety of exaggerated hand gestures.

Strozzi's picture is closely related to an altarpiece of the same subject painted around 1598 in Rome by Caravaggio, the influential painter who popularized the use of dramatic lighting effects. It is not known whether Strozzi, a native of Genoa, ever traveled to Rome to see the painting by Caravaggio; he may have known it only through copies and reports of other artists.   —JAW

GUERCINO (GIOVANNI FRANCESCO BARBIERI)

Italian, 1591–1666
Domestic Conflict, about 1630
Pen and brown ink drawing with wash
on cream laid paper
11⅛ × 10⅜ in. (28.8 × 26.4 cm) sheet
Museum purchase, 1951.21

Despite a humble birth in a small farming village in northern Italy, Guercino worked his way up to the employ of the pope and then became the leading painter of Bologna. Known from childhood by the nickname "Guercino" (the squinter) because of his cross-eyed appearance, he was the era's most prolific and eloquent draftsman. In addition to preparatory drawings for paintings, he drew landscapes, momentary sketches of everyday life, and even caricatures. Favoring pen and ink to record fleeting glimpses of activity, Guercino preferred to use flexible feather-quill pens, and he probably made his own inks from fireplace ashes or from insect galls on trees. The ink on this sheet was so acidic that it ate away the paper where the drawn lines were densest.

For many years called *The Enraged Husband,* this drawing has a spontaneous, anecdotal quality common to many of Guercino's sketches. It is likely that it represents a scene from a popular play.　　—DA

JUDITH LEYSTER
Dutch, 1609–60
A Game of Tric-Trac, about 1630
Oil on panel
16½ × 12¼ in. (40.7 × 31.1 cm)
Gift of Robert and Mary S. Cushman,
1983.58

Leyster is the only woman painter from Holland's Golden Age whose artistic production indicates an active role in the open art market. A native of Haarlem, she painted almost all of her known works there before her marriage to another local painter, Jan Miense Molenaer. The subjects of Leyster's paintings are taken from everyday life to make the kind of pictures that were in demand as private individuals began to replace the Church and the state as artists' chief clients. Backgammon, or tric-trac, as the game was commonly called, was a popular pastime in Leyster's day. Here the artist engages the viewer through the dramatic pose of the figure on the left. The female player, who may well be a courtesan, holds a glass of wine and offers her partner a clay smoking pipe. Drinking and smoking, like tric-trac, were considered idle pursuits in seventeenth-century Holland. The artificial light, which helps to focus our attention on these "vices," also emphasizes the element of seduction.

—JAW

ALONSO CANO
Spanish, 1601–67
Christ Bearing the Cross,
about 1635–37
Oil on canvas
65½ × 39¾ in. (166.5 × 101 cm)
Museum purchase, 1920.95

A painter, sculptor, and architect, Cano trained under the prominent teacher Francisco Pacheco in Seville, the home of Spain's most important Baroque painters. Like his fellow student Diego Velázquez, who rose to become the great master of this age, Cano was called to Madrid to work at the court of Philip IV. This painting, probably completed shortly before Cano's move to Madrid, once hung in the Colegio de San Alberto in Seville. The subject of Christ carrying the cross was a popular one in Spain and even today is often acted out as part of religious ritual. Cano drew attention to the suffering Christ through realistic details like the rope around his neck, the crown of thorns on his head, and his blood-stained brow. The realism is heightened by strong contrasts of light and shadow, a technique that ultimately derives from the influential Italian Baroque master Caravaggio. These dramatic effects were favored by many artists of the Counter Reformation, who used them to engage the viewer in their subjects.   —JAW

DANIEL SEGHERS and ERASMUS
QUELLINUS II
>Flemish, 1590–1661 and 1607–78
>*A Garland of Flowers with the Education
>of the Virgin,* about 1645
>Oil on canvas
>47⁷⁄₁₆ × 37 in. (112.5 × 94 cm)
>Eliza S. Paine Fund in memory of
>William R. and Frances T. C. Paine, 1966.37

During the seventeenth century, when Netherlandish painters often specialized in certain
subjects, it was not uncommon for two or
more artists to collaborate on a single work.
In this picture the flowers were painted by
Seghers and the sculptured stone cartouche by
Quellinus, who is known to have worked with
Seghers on several occasions. Seghers, a Jesuit
monk, learned his specialty of floral garlands

in the studio of his teacher, Jan Brueghel. A
favorite of Flemish painters, these colorful
clusters were often enhanced by being placed
against monochromatic backgrounds. Here the
garland contains almost two dozen different
floral species and a variety of butterflies, at-
testing to the growing interest in document-
ing the natural world. The attention lavished
on the garland gives it precedence over the
painting's central subject, the Virgin with
her mother, Saint Anne. Close examination
reveals that the seated figure originally held
the Christ Child on her lap and therefore represented the Virgin Mary. When the child was
painted out and the standing figure was added,
the subject became the Education of the Virgin.

—JAW

MICHAEL SWEERTS
Flemish, 1624–64
A Young Couple and a Boy in a Garden,
about 1650
Oil on canvas
14⅞ × 19³⁄₁₆ in. (37.7 × 48.8 cm)
Charlotte E. W. Buffington Fund, 1961.40

A native of Brussels, Sweerts was one of the many seventeenth-century Netherlandish artists who spent time in Rome, where he painted primarily "low-life" genre scenes. This work, done around the midpoint of his ten-year stay there, shows the influence of Caravaggio, the Italian painter who first popularized the use of strong contrasts of light and shadow to create dramatic effects. Sweerts's paintings appear to have been made primarily for private collectors, who often preferred pictures of this moderate scale for display in their homes.

Many paintings from this period that appear to be a reflection of daily life are filled with further meaning. While we cannot be sure of the full message of this painting, its setting—an enclosed garden—is a traditional sexual symbol, as is the bunch of grapes the man holds. The woman's décolleté costume suggests that she may be a courtesan.

—JAW

JAN STEEN

Dutch, 1625/6–79
The Rhetoricians, about 1655
Oil on panel
28⅜ × 23⅝ in. (72 × 60 cm)
Eliza S. Paine Fund in memory of William R. and Frances T. C. Paine, 1954.22

One of the most prolific artists of his day, Steen has left us some of the most vivid portrayals of the social life he witnessed, often with humorous or moralistic overtones. The men depicted here are probably members of the guild of Rhetoricians (*Rederijkers*), a group of poets and dramatists who banded together for fellowship, readings, and theatrical performances. These organizations, which could be found in the major towns of seventeenth-century Holland, were often the subject of paintings from the period. Here the prominent coat of arms hanging from the sill bears the emblem of the Amsterdam guild of Rhetoricians called "Egelantiers," a flowering eglantine, and their motto, "flourishing in love" (*in liefde bloeinende*). The man on the right wearing a beret has been identified as Steen, who frequently included himself in his paintings. As far as we know, he was never a member of the Egelantiers.   —JAW

GIOVANNI BENEDETTO CASTIGLIONE
Italian, about 1609–64
A Satyr Family among Animals, about 1650
Oil and ink drawing on cream laid paper
11 9/16 × 17 9/16 in. (29.4 × 44.6 cm) sheet
Museum purchase, 1956.38

One of the greatest Baroque masters in the northern Italian port city of Genoa, Castiglione trained in his hometown under both animal and landscape painters. His distinctive personal style is characterized by energized, lively handling of the brush and drawing stylus. Oil sketches by the Flemish painters Anthony van Dyck and Peter Paul Rubens may have inspired his loosely executed paintings and helped him develop the spirited manner that he maintained throughout his career. Many of Castiglione's paintings and prints represent zoolike arrays of animals. Some depict the loading of Noah's ark, while others, like this example, are scenes from classical mythology. Its finish and density suggest that this is one of Castiglione's earliest surviving color oil sketches.   —DA

JACOB VAN RUISDAEL
Dutch, about 1628/9–82
View on the IJ on a Stormy Day, about 1660
Oil on canvas
25 ⅞ × 32 ⁹⁄₁₆ in. (65.8 × 82.7 cm)
Theodore T. and Mary G. Ellis Collection,
1940.52

The most celebrated of the Dutch landscape painters, Ruisdael also painted a number of impressive seascapes, all of which appear to date after 1656, when he had left his hometown of Haarlem and settled in Amsterdam, Holland's largest city. In this example he focused on the IJ, the arm of the Zuider Zee that forms the harbor of Amsterdam, just barely visible on the horizon at the left. Ruisdael's main interest was the force of nature, indicated by the agitated water and ominous sky. In the movement of the clouds overhead, we can almost feel the wind blowing across the sea or anticipate a sudden shift in the pattern of light and shadow on the water. Like so many of his contemporaries, Ruisdael used his art to comment on nature's transitoriness, and in this case, the carefully placed sailing vessels, dwarfed against the vast sky, suggest man's subservience to the atmospheric elements.   —JAW

PIETER SAENREDAM
Dutch, 1597–1665
Interior of the Choir of Saint Bavo's Church at Haarlem, 1660
Oil on panel
27¹¹⁄₁₆ × 21⁹⁄₁₆ in. (70.4 × 54.8 cm)
Charlotte E. W. Buffington Fund, 1951.29

Saenredam spent most of his life in Haarlem, where he painted this interior view of the town's main church (which would become his burial site). The structure, originally built by Catholics, was converted to a Dutch Reformed Church in the late sixteenth century, when Protestantism became the dominant religion in the northern Netherlands. The simplicity of the church interior was dictated by Protestant emphasis on the word rather than visual adornment.

Saint Bavo's today remains much as it was depicted by Saenredam, the first Dutch artist to specialize in faithful renderings of specific buildings. His method of working was careful and accurate. He would first make a detailed sketch on the site, followed by an even more precise construction drawing, often with the help of measurements and plans. The initial sketch for the Worcester painting is preserved in Weimar, Germany.   —JAW

JOB BERCKHEYDE
Dutch, 1630–93
The Baker, about 1681
Oil on canvas
24 ¹⁵/₁₆ × 20 ⅞ in. (63.4 × 53 cm)
Gift of Mr. and Mrs. Milton P. Higgins,
1975.105

A specialist in cityscapes, Berckheyde painted several pictures of bakery shops, which were popular as a subject for Dutch artists from around 1650. This inviting scene shows the baker blowing a horn to announce the morning's freshly baked bread. He is surrounded by a mouth-watering assortment of goods, including pretzels displayed on a specially designed wooden rack.

The number of bakeries was considerable in seventeenth-century Holland, and like most merchants, bakers usually set up their operations in their own homes. Because their ovens were considered fire threats to adjacent property, they were often forced to live and do business in stone buildings, which probably explains Berckheyde's choice of architecture for *The Baker.* As for the model he selected, while an artist would have had no difficulty finding a real baker to pose, Berckheyde, it seems, painted himself in the role.   —JAW

BACICCIO (GIOVANNI BATTISTA
GAULLI)
    Italian, 1639–1709
    Vision of Saint Ignatius at La Storta, about
    1684–85
    Oil on canvas
    28¼ × 14⅛ in. (71.7 × 36 cm)
    Charlotte E. W. Buffington Fund, 1974.298

This painting is thought to be a model for a
large altarpiece intended for Sant' Ignatio,
one of the major Jesuit churches in Rome. The
final commission, however, appears never to
have been completed. Appropriately, the subject represents a key event in the life of Saint
Ignatius, the founder of the Jesuit order. In
1537, while on his way to Rome, Ignatius

had a vision in which God the Father and
Christ instructed him to establish a religious
community in that city. The Jesuit order grew
dramatically, helping to spread the influence
of the Catholic Church around the world during the late sixteenth and seventeenth century, the period of the Counter Reformation.
Toward the end of that time Baciccio became
one of the most prominent painters in Rome.
His skill at depicting mystical visions makes
him one of the masters of Italian Baroque art.

—JAW

HYACINTHE RIGAUD
French, 1659–1743
Portrait of Charles-Auguste d'Allonville,
Marquis de Louville, 1708
Oil on canvas
55 ½ × 42 ¹⁵⁄₁₆ in. (141 × 109 cm)
Charlotte E. W. Buffington Fund and
Eliza S. Paine Fund, 1980.35

Painter to the courts of both Louis XIV and
Louis XV, Rigaud was the favorite portraitist of royalty and nobility during the late
seventeenth and early eighteenth century.
Extremely prolific, he executed hundreds
of portraits of nobles, diplomats, military
leaders, and monarchs, including a famous
full-length likeness of Louis XIV, now at
Versailles. The subject of the Worcester picture is Charles-Auguste d'Allonville, who
held numerous titles, including Head of the
House of Philip V, the first Bourbon king of
Spain. In 1708, the year the marquis was
married, Rigaud painted pendant portraits—
this painting and one of the nobleman's wife
(still in a private collection)—probably in
commemoration of their wedding. As in most
of Rigaud's portraits, the emphasis is on the
subject's social rank, here conveyed by the
commanding pose and elaborate costume.

—JAW

JEAN-BAPTISTE PATER
French, 1695–1736
The Dance, about 1730
Oil on canvas
38⅛ × 51¼ in. (96.9 × 130.2 cm)
Museum purchase, 1942.53

Pater studied with the great eighteenth-century master Jean-Antoine Watteau, from whose work he often borrowed. Like Watteau, he favored the theme known as *fête galante*, a romantic grouping of elegant figures within a dreamlike landscape. These paintings reflect a shift in French art from the grand and stately Baroque manner of the seventeenth century to the more intimate and refined style of the early eighteenth century known as Rococo. By this time painting was no longer primar-ily a court art but an art of society, and the interaction between men and women was often treated in a lighthearted manner, as in *The Dance*.

As the number of paintings commissioned by private patrons increased during the Rococo period, many artists repeated the same theme. Pater, despite this repetition, always main-tained a sensitive handling of delicate colors and a penchant for careful detail, especially in the figures. —JAW

WILLIAM HOGARTH
British, 1697–1764
William James, 1744
Mrs. William James, 1744
Oil on canvas
29¾ × 25 in. (75.6 × 63.5 cm)
30 × 25 in. (76.2 × 63.5 cm)
Museum purchases, 1910.3 and 1910.4

During the sixteenth and seventeenth century, British painting was dominated by foreign masters, particularly Dutch and Flemish. It was not until the eighteenth century that the English began to rival the work of their contemporaries from the Continent. One of the great masters of this period was William Hogarth, best known for biting satires of society that were popularized in now-famous engravings. He was also skilled as a portraitist, capable of capturing the true character of his sitters. In this pair of portraits, he suggested the confidence of the country squire William James (1704–81), who had been High Sheriff of Kent in 1732 at the age of twenty-eight, and the somewhat naïve, but refreshing, demeanor of his young wife, Elizabeth (died 1798). Proud of their fine London fashions, the two are shown in an oval format, which perhaps reflects the influence of Hogarth's visit to Paris the preceding year.

—JAW

FRANÇOIS BOUCHER
French, 1703–70
The Annunciation, about 1749
Black chalk drawing on cream laid paper
13 9/16 × 8 1/8 in. (34.4 × 20.7 cm) sheet
Eliza S. Paine Fund, 1976.3

A celebrated artist in his day, Boucher was favored by his mistress Madame de Pompadour. He gained further renown as a superb, versatile draftsman, and his drawings in many different media were highly regarded by collectors during his lifetime. In both painting and drawing Boucher treated a great diversity of subjects, including mythology, nudes, landscapes, genre scenes, and portraits. To his contemporaries Boucher's theatrical realm of sensuous make-believe seemed appropriate for such worldly themes yet less suitable for religious topics. His drawings of sacred subjects —made chiefly for himself—far outnumbered his paintings.

Worcester's drawing shows the Archangel Gabriel hovering near Mary, to announce to her that she will bear the Son of God. Above, reclining on a cloud like a pagan divinity, God the Father releases the Dove of the Holy Spirit. The rounded top of the drawing suggests that it may have been a design for an altarpiece, perhaps a preliminary sketch, as indicated by the loose handling of the black chalk. —AD

JEAN-BAPTISTE GREUZE
French, 1725–1805
Le Geste Napolitain, 1757
Oil on canvas
28¾ × 37⅛ in. (73 × 94.3 cm)
Charlotte E. W. Buffington Fund, 1964.113

Greuze won success in the 1760s, when he
began exhibiting scenes from the lives of
ordinary citizens designed to teach a moral
lesson. These story-telling compositions often
incorporated figures in dramatic and "staged"
poses that had heretofore been reserved for
loftier historical and religious subjects. The
subject of Worcester's painting is typical of
Greuze's narrative compositions, intricately
conceived and imbued with romantic and sen-
timental overtones. While the precise meaning of the scene is unclear, there is no doubt
that Greuze intended a moralistic message.

With a brokenhearted look and a "Nea-
politan gesture" of dismissal, the young
woman seems to send away the man dressed
as a peddler; that his tradesman's costume is
a disguise is clear from the cross of nobility
he wears. Each figure's face expresses a particular reaction to the moment, including
the old woman who tries to intervene and
the two children at the lower right, one of
whom attempts to restrain the barking dog.
A superb draftsman, Greuze incorporated
elements of still life such as the peddler's
basket of colorful threads and sewing material and the ceramic pot and basket on the
plinth at the right.   —JAW

PIETRO LONGHI
  Italian, 1702–85
  Visit to a Library, about 1760
  Oil on canvas
  23 ¼ × 17 ½ in. (59 × 44.3 cm)
  Museum purchase, 1942.2

Longhi was one of the most popular artists in eighteenth-century Venice. Turning away from expansive historical and religious subjects, he devoted himself to detailed scenes of contemporary life. Like the work of two French counterparts, Nicolas Lancret and Jean-Antoine Watteau, his art reflects growing attacks on societal conventions, which became one of the hallmarks of the Age of Enlightenment. Here, portraying elegantly dressed visitors to a library as somewhat frivolous, Longhi ably captured the graceful decay of the Venetian republic. A gently ironic portrait of fashionable aristocracy, the painting is executed in subtle tones of yellow, silver, and pink against a neutral background.

—JAW

THOMAS GAINSBOROUGH
    British, 1727–88
    Portrait of the Artist's Daughters,
    about 1763–64
    Oil on canvas
    50⅛ × 40⅟₁₆ in. (127.2 × 101.7 cm)
    Museum purchase, 1917.181

Gainsborough's two daughters were among his favorite subjects. He painted at least five double and several individual portraits of them at various ages. Here he suggested his daughters' interest in his own profession by showing them holding drawing materials and next to two classical sculptures. X rays of the painting reveal that Margaret stood originally on the left side of the composition, opposite her older sister, Mary. By repositioning her,

Gainsborough stressed the close relationship between the two girls—a quality that can be seen also in his other portraits of them.

Along with Sir Joshua Reynolds, Gainsborough was instrumental in raising British portrait painting to a level comparable to that found much earlier on the Continent. Influenced by earlier French and Netherlandish art, especially the portraiture of Anthony van Dyck, Gainsborough incorporated elegance and expressive brushwork into his portraits, making him a favorite among England's aristocratic class.   —JAW

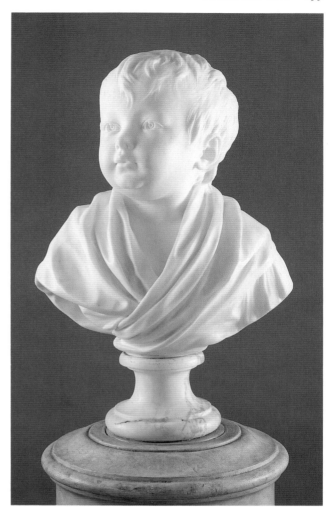

JEAN-ANTOINE HOUDON
French, 1741–1828
Claudine Houdon, about 1791
Marble
H: 9¾ in. (24.7 cm) W: 11½ in. (29.2 cm)
D: 7⅝ in. (19.4 cm)
Stoddard Acquisition Fund, 1964.17

Recognized as one of the greatest portrait sculptors of all times, Houdon worked in the neoclassical style. In his early twenties he spent four years in Italy studying the art of the antique. Back in Paris he quickly became famous for portrait sculpture and received commissions from all over the world. His subjects ranged from the French philosophers Diderot, Voltaire and Rousseau to the American patriots Washington, Jefferson, and Lafayette. These carefully crafted portraits capture not only the physiognomy but also the character of the sitters. In portraits of his wife and children Houdon achieved an added measure of intimacy and warmth, as in this charming bust of his third daughter, Claudine, who was about a year old at the time.

—JAW

PHILIBERT-LOUIS DEBUCOURT
French, 1755–1832
La Promenade Publique, 1792
Etching, engraving, mezzotint, and
aquatint on cream laid paper
14 × 23 in. (35.5 × 58.4 cm) plate
Gift of Mrs. Kingsmill Marrs, 1925.154

Debucourt trained as a painter at the French
Academy and exhibited pictures at its official Salon throughout his career. In the 1780s
he began experimenting with color intaglio
prints that reproduced his own compositions
representing the elegant lives of the French
nobility in the years before the Revolution.
Most of the prints he made later were repro-
ductions after the designs of other artists.

La Promenade Publique was inspired by
Vauxhall Gardens, a print made in London in
1785 by Thomas Rowlandson, which was an
instant success on both sides of the channel.

Partly society fashion plate and partly gossipy
caricature, that large color aquatint depicted
the celebrities and the upper crust of cosmopolitan London parading themselves at the
city's most famous night spot. By the time
Debucourt produced this, his own French
version, seven years later, he had become
interested in new printmaking techniques
that simulate the look of watercolor paintings. His achievement here is the last and
perhaps the greatest French color print of
the eighteenth century. Engaging in its
satire, the print is also provocative in fore-
shadowing the massacres of the French
nobility in September 1792.   —DA

GRAINGER, LEE AND COMPANY, WORCESTER

British, 19th century
Fruit Cooler, about 1820
Porcelain
H: 13 3/16 in. (33.5 cm) W: 12 1/8 in. (30.8 cm)
DIAM: 9 3/8 in. (23.8 cm)
Theodore T. and Mary G. Ellis Collection,
1940.205g

Painted on the front panel of this fruit cooler is a view of England's great Worcester Cathedral with its fourteenth-century Gothic tower rising beyond the Severn Bridge; at the left are other landmarks—probably the tower of Saint Swithin's Church and the spire of Saint Andrew's Church. Exotic birds in a river landscape are pictured on the reverse panel. The dark blue urn-shaped vessel with gilt decoration comes from an English city noted for its fine porcelain ware. Worcester became a center for porcelain manufacture with the establishment in 1751 of the Worcester Porcelain Company, whose success gave rise to the creation of other such firms in the nineteenth century. The product of a competitive manufacturer, the cooler is from a dessert service made about 1820 by Grainger, Lee and Company, in business from 1812 to 1837. Thomas Grainger, a partner who had worked prior to 1801 as a ceramic artist for the Chamberlain factory at Worcester, saw to it that Grainger, Lee and Company became a leading source for richly decorated porcelain.   —SBJ

Monstrosities of 1822 — Pl. 5.

GEORGE CRUIKSHANK
> British, 1792–1878
> *Monstrosities of 1822—Part 5,* 1822
> Etching with watercolor on cream
> wove paper
> 10 3/16 × 14 3/4 in. (25.9 × 37.6 cm) plate
> Dr. Samuel B. Woodward Collection,
> 1934.123

The work of Cruikshank represents the culmination of a long British tradition of satirical prints, which enjoyed popularity from the mid-eighteenth to the mid-nineteenth century. As the leading political and social caricaturist of his day, he criticized myriad aspects of London life at all levels of society. Cruikshank delighted in poking fun at contemporary fashions. In his *Monstrosities*— a series of nine prints executed between 1816 and 1827—he lambasted the sartorial absurdities of the Regency, the heyday of dandies like Beau Brummel. This etching shows a promenade of dandified strutters thronging beneath the statue of a resplendent male nude.

The Worcester Art Museum's collection of works by Cruikshank is particularly rich, containing over two thousand prints and illustrated books. All were given to the Museum in 1934 by Dr. Samuel B. Woodward.

—AD

El famoso Americano, Mariano Ceballos

FRANCISCO JOSÉ DE GOYA Y LUCIENTES

Spanish, 1746–1828
The Celebrated American, Mariano Ceballos, from the series *The Bulls of Bordeaux,* 1825
Lithograph on cream wove paper
12 ¹⁵⁄₁₆ × 16 ⅛ in. (31.2 × 40.9 cm) image
Bequest of Mrs. Kingsmill Marrs, 1926.682

Portraitist, muralist, genre and history painter, and printmaker, Goya was a political and social moralist whose art often castigated the repressive Spanish monarchy. Following a revolt by liberals in 1820, which reestablished a constitutional government, the absolutist Bourbon king Fernando VII regained power in 1823. In 1824 the disillusioned Goya went into exile in Bordeaux, France. There he made a set of four large lithographs of bullfighting scenes. Eight years before he had created a series of thirty-three etchings and aquatints called *Tauromaquia* that constitute a tribute to this popular Spanish pastime. Working in the recently developed medium of lithography, the aged artist, who could barely see, drew entirely from memory, using a crayon directly on the lithographic stones.

This print shows the Argentine matador about to strike a bull with a short sword. Through scraping, Goya blurred the contours of the beast that Ceballos rides, thus intensifying the dynamism of its movement. A similar economy of means defines the spectators, whose forms emerge in a scintillating texture of light and shadow. —AD

JEAN-BAPTISTE JOSEPH WICAR
French, 1762–1834
*Electra Receiving the Ashes of Her
Brother, Orestes*, 1826–27
Oil on canvas
39¹¹⁄₁₆ × 53¾ in. (100.8 × 136.5 cm)
Stoddard Acquisition Fund, 1991.47

During the late eighteenth and early nineteenth century, when European artists were influenced stylistically by the art of ancient Greece and Rome, they also focused on subjects from classical literature. Sophocles's *Electra* inspired this work depicting an encounter between Electra and her brother, Orestes, whom she had believed to be dead. Bearing a funerary urn, he has returned in disguise to his homeland after an absence of many years to avenge the murder of his father, Agamemnon, whose tomb can be seen at the left. Clytemnestra, the mother of Electra and Orestes, who was responsible for her husband's death, appears at the far right with her lover, Aegisthus.

A native of Lille, Wicar studied in Paris with the leading painter of the neoclassical style, Jacques-Louis David. By 1800 Wicar had settled in Rome, where he painted this canvas for the French ambassador to that city.

—JAW

DAVID OCTAVIUS HILL and
ROBERT ADAMSON
> British, 1802–70 and 1821–48, respectively
> *Group of Six Gentlemen, Edinburgh,* 1843
> Calotype
> 9¼ × 11¹¹⁄₁₆ in. (23.5 × 29.7 cm)
> Gift of Mrs. Roger Kinnicutt, 1966.50

The calotype, a negative-positive process patented in 1841 by William Henry Fox Talbot (1800–77), takes its name from the Greek word for beauty, *kalos*. Hill, a painter and secretary of the Royal Scottish Academy, employed the new photographic technique to make portrait studies as a preliminary step in creating a monumental work in oils. The painting (now in the collection of the Free Church of Scotland) commemorates a church convention in 1843 that severed ties with the British Crown to found the Free Church of Scotland. Hill sought the collaboration of Adamson, a Saint Andrews calotypist, to photograph the individual church delegates—among them the professor and one of the five ministers shown here. This "indoor" scene was actually staged outdoors to utilize sunlight for making the one- to two-minute exposure required to produce a satisfactory paper negative. It was one of fifteen hundred photographs—including portraits, architectural subjects, and seaside scenes—the two artists took during a five-year period before their partnership ended with Adamson's death in 1848.   —SBJ

JEAN-AUGUSTE-DOMINIQUE INGRES
French, 1780–1867
Study for a Portrait of Madame Moitessier,
about 1844–49
Black and red chalk drawing on white
wove paper
14 × 12³⁄₁₆ in. (35.5 × 30.9 cm) sheet
In memory of Mary Alexander Riley with
funds given by her friends, 1964.82

The leader of the classical school of French painting from the 1820s through the 1860s, Ingres was acclaimed for his exquisite draftsmanship and his penetrating insight into the human personality. In 1844 he was commissioned to execute a portrait of Madame Marie-Clotilde-Inès de Foucauld Moitessier, daughter of a government functionary, whose beauty the artist considered divine. This painting (in the National Gallery, London), which troubled Ingres for many years, was completed only in 1856; it shows her seated in a majestic pose derived from a female figure in an ancient Roman fresco from Herculaneum, which Ingres had probably viewed in Naples as a young artist. In 1851, when this commission was still unfinished, he responded to his client's polite prodding with a portrait of her standing (in the National Gallery of Art, Washington, D.C.).

Worcester's drawing—a study for the London painting—shows the head and hand in the same position as those in the Roman figure. The artist's superb handling of black and red chalks creates firm contours, delicate tonal nuances, and subtle facial animation. Abbreviated though it is, the sketch suggests Ingres's idealization of form and the love of the antique that underlie his art.   —AD

JEAN-FRANÇOIS MILLET

French, 1814–75
Bringing Home the Newborn Calf,
about 1857–58
Charcoal drawing with white heightening
on cream wove paper
10⅝ × 12¾ in. (27 × 32.3 cm) sheet
Gift of Mrs. Howard W. Preston, 1974.329

Millet's rural images must be understood in the context of societal transformation after the Revolution of 1848 in Paris. In the political upheavals of that event, peasants emerged as symbols of a simpler, preindustrial life, and for intellectual radicals they also embodied aspirations for social change in an urban, industrial world. Fleeing the turmoil of Paris in 1849, Millet moved to the village of Barbizon to devote his energies to rendering scenes of the country. The present drawing was stimulated by one of the artist's rare trips to other locales, a visit to his Norman birthplace of Gruchy in 1854. This rather finished work is one of several that he made in the following years, all leading up to a painting of 1864 (now in the Art Institute of Chicago).

Combining a naturalism born of direct observation with submerged references to classical and biblical themes in earlier art, Millet elevated genre scenes to a high level of seriousness. In their ponderousness and almost ritual solemnity, these farmers carrying a newborn calf resemble processions in paintings by such earlier masters as Nicolas Poussin and Pieter Brueghel. Although the painter's champions interpreted his pictures as emblems of hope and as tools of social reform, Millet himself viewed the peasant as fatally trapped in an oppressive cycle.

—AD

GUSTAVE COURBET
French, 1819–77
Woman with a Cat, 1864
Oil on canvas
28⅞ × 22½ in. (73.3 × 57 cm)
Museum purchase, 1940.300

A champion of the Realist movement of the mid-nineteenth century, Courbet chose subjects from everyday life. His main purpose was to draw attention to the world around him, as opposed to the idyllic and romantic themes of earlier generations. To stress his new style, Courbet often attempted to shock his audiences, painting a number of works with erotic overtones that challenged the standards of decorum at that time. Here sensuality is implied by the combination of a playful cat and the coquettish glance of the woman in a morning cap. Equally bold is the artist's technique, consisting of rapid brushwork that was a major break from the refined style of the academic tradition and a forerunner of Impressionism.

—JAW

CHARLES NÈGRE
  French, 1820–80
  Harvesters near Grasse, 1865
  Albumen print
  DIAM: 5 ¹⁵⁄₁₆ in. (15 cm)
  Stoddard Acquisition Fund, 1990.16

Nègre's reputation as a photographer rests on his genre pictures of Paris street life and on his landscape and architectural views of the Midi. Trained as a painter in the Paris studio of Paul Delaroche, he looked to his contemporaries for inspiration as he created authentic views of the rural world near his birthplace, Grasse, in southern France. This photograph recalls similar subjects by Jean-François Millet, a Barbizon artist who depicted country life realistically in his paintings and graphic work. Cropped from a rectangular negative, the picture's circular format unifies foreground and background—the workers in the field with haystacks, the poplar trees, and the distant landscape.   —SBJ

SIR EDWARD COLEY BURNE-JONES
British, 1833–98
Earth Mother, 1882
Encaustic on panel
17 5/16 × 10 5/8 in. (44 × 27 cm)
Sarah C. Garver and Charlotte E. W.
Buffington Funds, 1983.1

Burne-Jones was a second-generation member of the Pre-Raphaelite artists, who rejected the growing materialization of industrialized England. Instead they focused on the comparative simplicity of the medieval world and the art of Italian painters prior to Raphael. *Earth Mother,* which shows the influence of Renaissance artists like Botticelli, was painted by Burne-Jones in connection with his series of stained-glass windows representing the planets. Here is an allusion to Earth Mother's role

of nurturing all life: human, represented by the child; animal, by the wolf; and horticultural, by the trees and vegetation. The snake next to the feet of Earth Mother symbolizes fertility and relates to Ceres, goddess of agriculture. To show earth's role in the transitional nature of water, the allegorical figure is represented holding up a blue jar that produces clouds, rain, and eventually a stream below. To create the ivorylike skin of the figures and the rich textures throughout, Burne-Jones employed the ancient technique of encaustic. The pigments are bound in a wax medium, over which the artist applied oil glazes and, in certain areas, minute touches of gold for an even more decorative effect.

—JAW

VINCENT VAN GOGH
>Dutch, 1853–90
>*Portrait of a Man in a Top Hat*, 1882
>Graphite drawing with white heightening
>on cream wove paper
>15 ¹¹⁄₁₆ × 9 ¹¹⁄₁₆ in. (39.9 × 24.6 cm) sheet
>Gift of Mr. and Mrs. Chapin Riley, in
>memory of Francis Henry Taylor, 1957.153

A prolific draftsman, van Gogh considered drawing to be the foundation of his art. Yet only in his work at The Hague and at Nuenen in the Netherlands, where he worked periodically in the early to mid-1880s, did he attach importance to sketching directly from the model. This image of an elderly man in a top hat is one of numerous studies of men from a workhouse in The Hague who posed for van Gogh in their everyday wear and in their Sunday best. The same man appears from a variety of angles in many drawings.

Here the subject is shown sporting a decoration on the left lapel of his overcoat and a badge bearing the numerals 399 on his right sleeve. The man's fragile dignity is suggested by his frail hand tugging at his coat and by his worn top hat. Van Gogh seems to have been attracted by the forceful physiognomy with outsize ears, ample whiskers, emphatically curving and pointed nose, and wizened mouth. Executed only two years after the artist had launched his career, this drawing reveals both his masterly touch and his human sympathies. The strong, nervous strokes on coarsely textured paper aptly convey the harshness of the poor man's existence.

—AD

PAUL CÉZANNE
French, 1839–1906
Study for The Cardplayers, 1890–92
Oil on canvas
12⅝ × 13⅞ in. (32 × 35.3 cm)
Museum purchase, 1931.104

Of all nineteenth-century painters, Cezanne has had the greatest influence on the major movements of modern art, from Cubism to Expressionism. A close contemporary of the leading French Impressionists, he strove to combine the lighter palette of these artists with a firmer rendering of form and space. Cézanne, who "re-created nature" by utilizing color and considerable distortion of form to express the essence of his subjects, often painted the same theme many times.

The Worcester canvas, one of a series of paintings depicting men engaged meditatively in a game of cards, is a study for a larger work consisting of three cardplayers (in the Metropolitan Museum of Art, New York). Working with small brushstrokes, Cézanne built up a complex organization of planes of color that define form and space. The result is a sense of monumentality even in this simple subject.   —JAW

PAUL GAUGUIN
French, 1848–1903
The Brooding Woman, 1891
Oil on canvas
35⅞ × 27 in. (91.2 × 68.7 cm)
Museum purchase, 1921.186

First a sailor, then a successful stockbroker in Paris, Gauguin began painting as a hobby in his mid-twenties. He soon allied himself with the Impressionist artists and exhibited with them from 1879 to 1886. In protest against the ills of civilization, he resolved to live primitively and eventually settled on the South Pacific island of Tahiti. This picture, painted during the first of two extended stays there, shows Gauguin's rejection of naturalism for stronger, unreal color and striking simplification of form, both of which had a strong influence on modern art of the early twentieth century. The silent and meditative subject of *The Brooding Woman* (translated from the original Tahitian title, *Te Faaturuma*) conveys the sense of mystery that the Polynesians evoked in the artist. He considered this painting among his best from the earlier Tahitian stay, and it was eventually acquired by the French Impressionist artist Edgar Degas, who owned a number of works by Gauguin.

—JAW

ANDERS ZORN
> Swedish, 1860–1920
> *Opal,* 1891
> Oil on canvas
> 38½ × 27⅜ in. (100.3 × 69.5 cm)
> Gift of Marianne and John Jeppson, 1986.89

Sweden's leading painter at the turn of the century, Zorn traveled and painted extensively, both in Europe and the United States; however, it was at Mora, his hometown, that he created some of his best works. The title of this picture refers to the rainbow of colors reflecting off the lake near Mora. Zorn took an informal approach to the traditional theme of the nude in the landscape by placing the figures at the left, looking into the distance. Working in the Impressionist style, he used pure, broken color to achieve brilliance and luminosity and free brushwork to convey the transitory nature of the subject. In this scene, which gives the impression of being painted directly from nature, the artist focused on the effects of light as it falls on the women and their lush surroundings.   —JAW

ODILON REDON
    French, 1840–1916
    The Wing, 1893
    Lithograph on *Chine appliqué*
    12⁹⁄₁₆ × 9⁹⁄₁₆ in. (32 × 24.4 cm) image
    Museum purchase, 1919.101

Though a contemporary of the Impressionists, Redon was one of the first artists to reject their scrutiny of optical effects in favor of exploring his own imaginary world. For the portrayal of his inner visions, he was admired at the turn of the century by the French Symbolists and by the Nabis, who sought to uncover the hidden aspects of life. Later, between the two world wars, the Surrealists hailed him as a forerunner. His strange and fantastic images are usually limited to one figure or object, often a winged creature, as in *The Wing*. This is one of several of his lithographs that represent Pegasus, the winged horse of Greek mythology.

Early in his career Redon renounced color and challenged himself to exploit the possibilities of charcoal, as he found it to be a medium that liberated his imagination and allowed him to focus on gradations of light and dark. To reproduce his drawings the artist turned in 1879 to lithography, attracted by the tonal effects that he could achieve with this printmaking process. During the next twenty years he worked chiefly in black and white, making over 170 lithographs. Only in the 1890s did he gradually turn to brilliantly colored works first in pastel, then color lithography and (after 1900) oil. —AD

FREDERICK H. EVANS
  British, 1853–1943
  Portrait of Aubrey Beardsley, 1894
  Platinum print
  4⅞ × 3⁹⁄₁₆ in. (12.4 × 9.1 cm)
  Jerome Wheelock Fund, 1966.58

A bookseller in London, Evans was a member of the Linked Ring, a group of dedicated amateurs who promoted photography as an art in Britain and abroad at the turn of the twentieth century. During a time when photographers retouched negatives and manipulated printing, he made "plain prints from plain negatives" and became well known for his evocative pictures of England's great cathedrals.

In 1889 Evans met Aubrey Beardsley (1872–98) and helped him to secure a commission from the publisher J. M. Dent to illustrate an edition of *Morte Darthur,* Sir Thomas Malory's legendary work. Mounted on a photographic copy of a decorative border drawn by Beardsley for Malory's book, this profile portrait emphasizes the delicate features of the twenty-one-year-old artist. The platinum paper used for the print was favored by art photographers of the time for its permanence and long gray scale.   —SBJ

PAUL SIGNAC
French, 1863–1935
Golfe Juan, 1896
Oil on canvas
25 ¾ × 32 in. (65.4 × 81.3 cm)
Gift from the Chapin and Mary Alexander
Riley Collection, 1964.27

Signac began his career as an Impressionist under the influence of Claude Monet. By 1884 he became associated with Georges Seu-rat, with whom he developed the the ories of Neo-Impressionism, a movement aimed at making Impressionism more sci-entific. Worcester's painting exhibits the technique called "Pointillism," a systematic refinement of Impressionism in which small dots of color are designed to fuse optically in the eye of the viewer into a vibrant hue. In contrast to the informality of the Impres-sionists, Signac created a carefully struc-tured design and gave greater definition to the various forms, silhouetted against the background. Framed by trees, his stylized composition depicts several identifiable land-marks of Golfe Juan in the south of France: from left to right, the lighthouse, the church of Saint Tropez, and the old Vauban fortress atop the hill.   —JAW

PABLO PICASSO
Spanish, 1881–1973
Portrait of Fernande Olivier, 1906
Drypoint on cream laid paper
6⅜ × 4⅝ in. (16.2 × 11.8 cm) plate
Sarah C. Garver Fund and anonymous
gifts, 1982.82

Throughout his remarkably long and prolific career, Picasso was an active printmaker who experimented with nearly all of the print media. After learning the techniques used by professional engravers and etchers in the autumn of 1904, he made about thirty prints over the next two years, probably with the assistance of the Parisian printer Auguste Delâtre. Translations into simple line of his "Rose Period" imagery, these etchings represent classicized naked youths on horseback or in sporting events, or the clowns or acrobats of traveling circuses. While the so-called *saltimbanque* prints have a certain quality of fantasy, detachment, and abstraction, Picasso's portraits convey heartfelt emotion. Such affection is apparent in his likeness of Fernande Olivier, the woman with whom he shared his life between 1904 and 1911. Only three other impressions of this rare drypoint are known. Olivier reproduced it for the frontispiece for her book *Picasso et ses amis (Picasso and His Friends),* a collection of anecdotal memoirs published in 1933.   —DA

GEORGES BRAQUE
> French, 1882–1963
> *Olive Trees,* 1907
> Oil on canvas
> 15 × 18¾₆ in. (38 × 46.3 cm)
> Gift from the Estate of Mrs. Aldus Chapin
> Higgins, 1970.122

Early in his career Braque was attracted to a group of painters who came to be known as Les Fauves (The Wild Beasts). Under the leadership of Henri Matisse and André Derain, the Fauvist painters worked in an expressive style characterized by bold distortion of forms and extremely intense colors. This painting was produced near the small French village of La Ciotat, a few miles east of Marseilles, where Braque took full advantage of the brilliant Mediterranean light. Unlike the preceding generation of artists—the Impressionists, who focused on capturing the natural effects of light and atmosphere—Braque and his contemporaries aimed at expressing their own feelings toward their subjects. The Worcester painting exhibits a wide range of dramatically intense colors that go far beyond an objective look at nature. After 1907 Braque took a different direction in art; and leaving behind the swirling lines, decorative colors, and subjective qualities of Fauvist paintings, he joined Picasso in pioneering the Cubist movement.

—JAW

CLAUDE MONET
French, 1840–1926
Water Lilies, 1908
Oil on canvas
37¼ × 35⅜ in. (94.7 × 89.9 cm)
Museum purchase, 1910.26

One of the leading French Impressionists, Monet began his career by painting mainly landscapes and cityscapes in which color and light were his primary concerns. By the 1890s he began to work in series, depicting the same subject in various seasons or at different hours of the day, to demonstrate how changes in atmosphere can affect the viewer's impression of the motif.

A favorite theme during the last two decades of Monet's life was the water-lily pond in his garden at Giverny. The Worcester canvas shows only the surface of the pond with its clusters of water lilies floating amid the reflection of sky and trees. Conveying the artist's idea of nature's ever-changing image, the indefinite and freely painted forms also point the way toward the more expressive painting techniques that have dominated much of twentieth-century art.   —JAW

OSKAR KOKOSCHKA
  Austrian, 1886–1980
  Portrait of an Italian Boy, about 1912
  Black ink applied with brush and watercolor
  drawing over charcoal on tan wove paper
  15 ¹³⁄₁₆ × 10 ¹³⁄₁₆ in. (40.2 × 27.5 cm) sheet
  Gift of Mrs. Alma Mahler-Werfel, 1959.112

Kokoschka emerged from the Art Nouveau influences dominant in Vienna in the early years of the twentieth century to become one of the foremost Expressionists in Berlin before World War I. While capturing the physical and psychological aspects of people he met, his portraits convey an emphatic personal response to them. Even in early portraits, such as this study, he was able to penetrate to the inner life of his subject. The exaggerated size of the Italian boy's eyes contributes to his soulful attitude and lends a haunting quality to the face. An enervated state is evoked through the nervous, agitated handling of contour lines and shading of forms, stylistic characteristics that derive from German Expressionism.

Kokoschka regarded drawing as self-revelatory, functioning much as a diary entry, allowing him to chronicle his experience and to fully grasp its significance. While the execution of this example appears to have been a spontaneous act, it is at the same time a final statement, capable of standing on its own as an independent work of art.   —AD

JACQUES VILLON
French, 1875–1963
Monsieur D. Reading, 1913
Drypoint on cream laid paper
15 5⁄16 × 11 9⁄16 in. (38.9 × 29.4 cm) plate
Museum purchase, 1953.85

Born Gaston Duchamp, Jacques Villon changed his name in 1895, when he resolved to become an artist. Sixteen years later he and his two brothers, Raymond Duchamp Villon and Marcel Duchamp, were involved in the rise of Cubism. Villon's turn to this movement marked a decisive shift in his work, which had consisted of posters lithographed in color, as well as etchings and aquatints depicting Parisian life at the turn of the century —all demonstrating affinities with the startling, fashionable images of his friend Henri de Toulouse-Lautrec. After 1911, Villon's organization of form into a precise, orderly web of lines and angles dominated his production for the rest of his life. In emulation of the austerity of his own Cubist paintings and those of Pablo Picasso and Georges Braque, Villon limited his graphic output to black and white.

Monsieur D. Reading represents the artist's father, Eusèbe Duchamp, whose half-length figure is broken into multiple crystalline facets in the Cubist manner. The ambiguity between solid and void makes it hard to distinguish the man's body from the surrounding atmosphere. A concern with movement and an interaction of light and shadow enliven the portrait.   —AD

HENRI MATISSE
French, 1869–1954
The Promenade, 1919
Oil on canvas
21 15/16 × 18 13/16 in. (55.7 × 47.7 cm)
Museum purchase, 1929.122

One of the most influential artists of the modern era, Matisse spearheaded the early twentieth-century movement known as Fauvism, which focused on a subjective use of color and form to express the inner feelings of the artist. Here the overall sketchlike quality conveys a relaxed mood appropriate for a Mediterranean subject. This picture was painted in Nice, where Matisse was attracted to the intensity of the light. The luminosity results primarily from applying the paint very thinly over a white ground, much of which is still visible. The artist's interest in decorative patterns is seen in the tile floor, balustrade, rippled sea, and distant foliage. Counterbalancing any sense of depth in the work, these freely rendered patterns serve to draw attention to the expressive nature of Matisse's art.

—JAW

MAX PECHSTEIN
German, 1881–1955
Dancer Reflected in a Mirror, 1923
Color woodcut on cream wove paper
19⁷⁄₁₆ × 15¾ in. (49.5 × 40.1 cm) image
Museum purchase (by exchange from
Louis W. Black), 1954.207

Pechstein was a Dresden-trained artist who
joined the German Expressionist circle called
Die Brücke (The Bridge) in 1906, a year after
the group had been started by Ernst Kirchner,
Erich Heckel, Karl Schmidt-Rotluff, and Fritz
Bleyl. Formed in reaction to Impressionism,
which these artists associated with bourgeois
values, the movement fostered the wide dis-
semination of art through prints, especially
woodcuts. The Brücke artists favored spontaneous execution, and by 1910 they had
evolved a signature style of colored, planar
forms.

Pechstein's woodcut of 1923, *Dancer Reflected in a Mirror,* reveals that the influence
of the Brücke continued to mark his work even
after World War I. Here the distortions of
form, bold carving of the woodblock, strident
colors, and roughness of ink application create
visual excitement and tension. Through these
harsh, even brutal stylistic qualities, Pechstein heightened the disturbing aspects of the
lewd subject matter: an automatonlike dancer
whose reflection in the mirror intensifies her
physical presence as she performs for leering
male onlookers. The theme of the dancer had
been important for the Brücke group before
the war, and for Pechstein there were personal
parallels. Like the dancer forced to prostitute
herself before an audience, he felt compelled
to produce art that met the demands of dealer
and public.   —AD

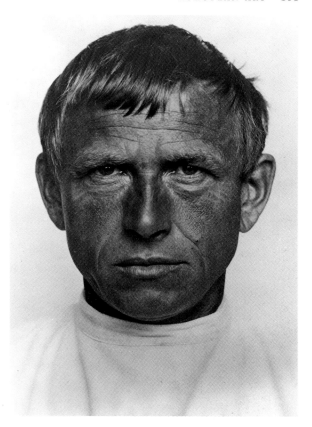

HUGO ERFURTH
German, 1874–1948
Otto Dix, about 1925
Gelatin silver print
6⁹⁄₁₆ × 4⁹⁄₁₆ in. (16.7 × 11.5 cm)
Stoddard Acquisition Fund, 1987.2

Erfurth and the painter Otto Dix (1891–1969) became close friends in the 1920s, when both artists lived in Dresden and created portraits of each other. Having absorbed the artistic concepts of nineteenth-century Realist portraiture early in his career, Erfurth carried that aesthetic into the Golden Twenties. Among the outstanding psychological studies he made of the Weimar Republic's citizenry from 1919 to 1933—people prominent in the arts, science, and politics—is this close-up photograph of Dix. The penetrating eyes reveal the keen intellect of a person accustomed to scrutinizing others as subjects for his art. Dix established himself in the 1920s as a leading figure of the Neue Sachlichkeit (New Objectivity) movement in which artists, reacting against Expressionism, depicted German life realistically with unflinching attention to detail.

—SBJ

WASSILY KANDINSKY
Russian, 1866–1944
Untitled painting, no. 629, 1936
Oil on canvas
51⅜ × 32 in. (130.5 × 81.4 cm)
Gift from the Estate of Mrs. Aldus Chapin
Higgins, 1970.123

Kandinsky emigrated from Russia to Munich, where he helped found the German Expressionist movement Der Blaue Reiter (The Blue Rider) in 1911. He soon became a pioneer of abstract art, eliminating recognizable objects and figures from his work. Kandinsky, who believed that art should not depend on its resemblance to nature (the two being separate entities), wrote of "what the spectator *lives* or *feels* while under the effect of the *form and color combinations* of the picture." A painting such as this one shows how, by improvising color and form according to his mood, he could create a world unto itself.

In several important treatises on art, Kandinsky often drew analogies between the visual arts and music. A teacher for several years at the Bauhaus, the famous German school of design, he has had a major effect on twentieth-century art.　　　　　　　　　　—JAW

BRASSAÏ (GYULA HALÁSZ)
French (born in Transylvania), 1899–1984
Gala Soirée at Maxim's, about 1946
Gelatin silver print
19½ × 15½ in. (49.5 × 39.4 cm)
Museum purchase, 1963.93

This photograph, taken in a fashionable Parisian restaurant just after World War II, captures the essence of a time when the rich, deprived of luxuries for six years, resumed their high living. Exposed in available light, the picture preserves the character of Maxim's restaurant, noted for its Art Nouveau decoration, and is the work of an artist who pioneered nighttime photography in the early 1930s. Brassaï gained recognition in the Parisian art world in 1933 with the publication of his first book of photographs, *Paris de Nuit,* which documents the night life of ordinary people in the city's cafés, dance halls, and streets. He made lifelong friendships with artists and literary figures whom he met in the cafés and photographed. Brassaï, who took his pseudonym from his native village, Brasso, in Transylvanian Hungary, was equally successful with other forms of artistic expression—painting, sculpture, and writing.

—SBJ

MATTA

French (born in Chile), 1911 or 1912
Untitled, 1962
Oil on canvas
69³⁄₁₆ × 78¹⁄₁₆ in. (175.7 × 198.3 cm)
Museum purchase, 1963.79

Roberto Sebastián Antonio Matta Echaurren was born in Chile to parents of French and Spanish descent. After receiving a degree in architecture, he moved to Paris to apprentice with the renowned French modernist architect Le Corbusier. Dissatisfied with his chosen field, Matta joined the circle of Surrealists around the poet André Breton in 1937 and within a year had begun painting. Between 1939 and 1948 he lived in New York, where he introduced Surrealist ideas to artists of the burgeoning New York School.

Whereas Matta's early Surrealist paintings depict inner landscapes of the artist's psyche, his later works reflect an interest in science and technology. This untitled work is a fantastical image—part futuristic science fiction, part nightmarish dreamscape—in which strange machines hover in an indeterminate space. Its cool, silver gray tonality punctuated by patches of warm orange reinforces the painting's eerie, cosmic quality.

—DH

Precolumbian Art

Standing Male Figure
about 800 B.C.
Mesoamerican, Olmec
Mexico (Veracruz)
Dark green stone
H: 5⅜ in. (13.6 cm) w: 2⅜ in. (6 cm)
D: 1⅝ in. (4.2 cm)
Museum purchase, 1958.32

Many of the practices and beliefs found throughout the ancient Mesoamerican cultures were initiated by the Olmec, who lived in the swampy lowlands of Veracruz. The first to evolve from simple village communities into a hierarchical society, the Olmec were governed by rulers with claims to divine authority. By the first millennium B.C. they had constructed large public ceremonial centers of massive architecture and displays of colossal sculptures.

Jade and similar green stones were among the most coveted commodities within the Olmec's extensive trade network. Valued for its rarity and beauty, green stone was often used to sculpt figurines for burial caches, such as the present example. This carved piece is a crude rendition of the man-jaguar, a figure whose meaning remains a mystery. While its downturned mouth and slanted eyes are typical features, the incised lines at the side of the mouth are unusual.　　　　—MPL

Urn with Human Figure
300 B.C.–A.D. 200
Mesoamerican, Zapotec
Mexico (Monte Albán)
Pottery with deposit of vermilion
H: 16 7/16 in. (42.1 cm) W: 8 in. (20.3 cm)
DIAM: 9 in. (22.8 cm)
Gift of Mrs. Aldus Chapin Higgins,
Mr. and Mrs. Ernest Angell, and
Mr. and Mrs. Milton P. Higgins in
memory of Aldus Chapin Higgins, 1961.37

The Zapotec arrived in the valley of Oaxaca in central Mexico by at least 500 B.C. and maintained their capital at Monte Albán until approximately A.D. 900. Despite evidence of extensive trade with other Mesoamericans, the Zapotec remained independent and developed their own writing system and artistic traditions. One typical Zapotec form is the cylindrical vessel with an effigy figure attached to the front. Placed in tombs and other architectural settings, these ceramic urns have been found empty for the most part; a few contained precious offerings of obsidian knives, green beads, and shells.

On this early example the figure wears a simple headdress of bells, woven cloth, and a small jaguar's head. Later urns are completely obscured by the effigy's elaborate ornamentation, mask, and headdress. While the exact significance of the urns remains unknown, their figures have been identified as deities or perhaps humans wearing the accoutrements of the gods and acting as intermediaries between the human and divine worlds.

—MPL

Model of a Ballgame
> 200 B.C.–A.D. 500
> Mesoamerican, Classic Maya
> Mexico (Nayarit)
> Pottery
> H: 6½ in. (16.5 cm) W: 14½ in. (36.8 cm)
> D: 10⅝ in. (27 cm)
> Gift of Mr. and Mrs. Aldus Chapin Higgins,
> 1947.25

Popular throughout Mexico, Central America, and northern South America from at least 1200 B.C. through the arrival of the Spanish in the sixteenth century was a ballgame in which players scored points by hitting a solid rubber ball past a marker without using their hands. In cultures such as the Classic Maya (A.D. 250–900), the game was a formal ritual with cosmological significance involving death and human sacrifice. The stone ballcourt represented the cosmos, the rubber ball the sun.

By engaging in the ballgame rituals and forcing weakened prisoners to play to the death, rulers reconfirmed their own prominent role among their people.

This dynamic scene from Nayarit in western Mexico is part of an artistic tradition of ceramic figures and clay scenes that were placed in deep shaft tombs as funerary offerings. The lively, crude rendition suggests simply a sporting event rather than a formal ritual.   —MPL

Flying-Panel Metate

A.D. 1–500
Central American
Costa Rica (Atlantic Watershed Region)
Stone
H: 17⅜ in. (44.2 cm) W: 34⅛ in. (87.3 cm)
D: 20⅞ in. (53 cm)
Museum purchase, 1965.3

While the peoples of Central America had contact with the major cultures of Mesoamerica and South America, they were not direct members of either sphere. Instead, they developed their own lively artistic traditions: stone and jade carving, ceramic sculpture, and goldworking. Among the burial offerings of the elite were basalt metates, or grinding stones —decorative forms of the staple item used in every household to grind maize and tubers. It is perhaps because of their crucial role in everyday existence that metates were elevated to the realm of the sacred by the people of Costa Rica. Using only stone and wood tools, they would carve a ritual metate from a single rock and decorate it with jaguars, birds, monkeys, and mythological creatures. In this example a free-hanging panel attached to only one leg is carved in the form of a large beaked bird with outstretched wings. Along the upper rim is a series of triangular incisions, a common abstract motif used to represent human heads.   —MPL

Portrait Vessel

A.D. 100–500
South American, Moche
Peru (North Coast)
Pottery painted red, buff, and black
H: 11⅛ in. (28.9 cm) W: 6½ in. (16.5 cm)
D: 5⁹⁄₁₆ in. (14.2 cm)
Museum purchase, 1968.55

The Moche civilization developed along the arid coastal plain of northern Peru. Through a vast network of irrigation channels, this people maintained control of fresh water, a rare commodity. In the eighth century, a series of natural catastrophes led to the downfall of the Moche. A vivid record remains of their achievement, however, in their ceramic vessels, a preferred form being the stirrup-spout bottle shown here. The bases of these bottles were fashioned into portraits of nobles, commoners, warriors, gods, animals, and plants. This portrait vessel is painted with typical red, buff, and black colors. A simple headband, tied under the young man's chin, is decorated with the full body of a jaguar or puma.   —MPL

Hacha
about A.D. 500
Mesoamerican, Classic Veracruz
Mexico (Veracruz)
Stone
H: 17 in. (43.3 cm) W: 3¾ in. (9.5 cm)
D: 6¹⁵⁄₁₆ in. (17.7 cm)
Eliza S. Paine Fund, 1963.68

Numerous existing artifacts from the central and northern parts of the state of Veracruz indicate a preoccupation with some form of ritual ballgame. A culture known as Classic Veracruz produced three kinds of stone objects symbolic of the actual equipment used in the game: yokes, *hachas* (axes), and *palmas* (long, narrow stones). Stone yokes are the ritual counterparts of leather-and-wood yokes worn around a player's waist to protect him from the heavy rubber ball. *Hachas* and *palmas* were set on the yoke, in front of the player, possibly to help control the ball or as a component of the ceremonial dress. *Hachas* may have been used also as markers along the sides of the court.

Scenes of death and the underworld, set within intricately carved scrolls, are common themes on these sculptures. Here a human face is framed by the curved jaws of an un-identified creature.   —MPL

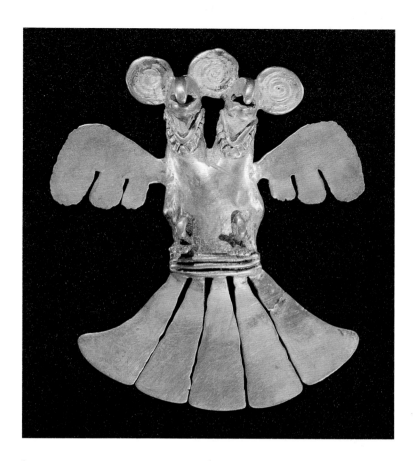

Double-Headed Eagle Pendant

A.D. 700–1500
South American, Popayán
Colombia
Gold
H: 2 13/16 in. (7.1 cm) W: 2 3/8 in. (6 cm)
D: 3/8 in. (.95 cm)
Museum purchase, 1959.82

While the peoples of Colombia developed individual artistic traditions, they shared many goldworking techniques and symbols in common with Central American artisans. The preferred metal for ornamentation was *tumbaga,* a gold-and-copper alloy used throughout the region to create a multitude of small figurines of birds, crabs, spiders, serpents, and anthropomorphic creatures. The figures were usually made by lost-wax casting and brightened by depletion gilding—a method in which the copper of the outermost surface was removed in an acid bath of organic materials, leaving a thin shell of pure gold.

This is an example of the so-called eagle pendant, an avian creature characterized by its large beak and widespread wings and tail. False filigree forms the head tufts, and wing and tail feathers have been emphasized by hammering and stretching the metal. Found frequently in Panama, the motif and style probably originated in Colombia and later spread northward.
—MPL

Carved Column
about A.D. 850
Mesoamerican, Classic Maya
Mexico (state of Campeche)
Limestone
H: 69 in. (175.3 cm) DIAM: 24 in. (61 cm)
Museum purchase, 1962.1

During the Classic period (A.D. 250–900), the Maya erected large stelae in ceremonial courtyards as public testimony to their divine authority. Often hieroglyphic text traced the ruler's royal lineage and commemorated important events such as birth, accession to power, or success in battle. This late Classic carving differs from its predecessors in that it lacks any text and it was not freestanding. One of the relatively rare round architectural columns from the Puuc region in the northern Maya lowlands, it dates from the transition period of Maya history when royal authority shifted from divine to secular sponsorship, military in nature. Here the ruler, dressed in the ceremonial garb of a warrior, carries a curved weapon in one hand; in the other is a shield decorated with the stylized face of the central Mexican rain god Tlaloc. The ruler's headdress is formed by the open jaws of the earth monster and is adorned with an abundance of feathers. Status is indicated by an enormous vest of jade squares and the high-backed sandals of the elite. More often presented alone, this ruler is accompanied by two dwarfs.   —MPL

Cup

A.D. 850–1050
South American, Sicán
Peru (North Coast)
Gold
H: 5⅜ in. (13.7 cm) DIAM: 4⅛ in. (10.5 cm)
Museum purchase, 1962.36

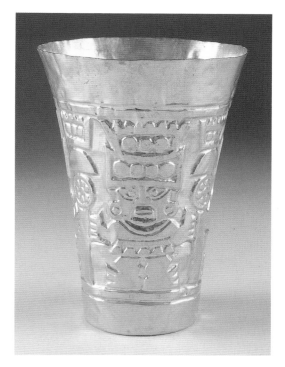

In the New World the art of metalworking
first began in South America, where there are
rich deposits of gold, silver, and copper. One of
the earliest pieces of hammered gold found in
the Peruvian highlands dates from 1500 B.C.
Because of its rarity and associations with the
sun, gold was reserved for nobility. The Sicán,
who established cities along the northern coast
of Peru in the late eighth century, buried their
elite with large quantities of precious objects,
including gold death masks and nested bea-
kers. This cup was created from a single sheet
of hammered gold, a favorite technique of the
craftsmen of the region. Its central figure, the
Lord of Sicán, is an ancient Andean icon associated with the sky deity. Here he is represented as a warrior and carries a spear in
each hand.   —MPL

Fertility Goddess
  1450–1521
  Mesoamerican, Aztec
  Mexico
  Stone with traces of pigment
  H: 13⅜ in. (34 cm) W: 6⅝ in. (16.9 cm)
  D: 4⅝ in. (11.8 cm)
  Museum purchase, 1957.143

Latecomers to the central valley of Mexico, arriving in the thirteenth century, the Aztecs soon conquered many of their neighbors and created a vast empire. Their capital, Tenochtitlán, now buried under Mexico City, supported over two hundred thousand inhabitants at the time of the Spanish Conquest in the early sixteenth century. The artistic achievements of the Aztec range from imposing monolithic stone sculpture to delicate featherwork. This small statue is one of the many representations of fertility deities found in stone sculptures and painted codices. She is adorned with two ears of corn in her hair, symbols of the maize goddess; a five-blossom headband and a jade necklace, attributes of the water goddess; and two signs of fertility: the double black stripes on her cheeks and a dusting of red pigment. Her pointed cape is unexpectedly plain.   —MPL

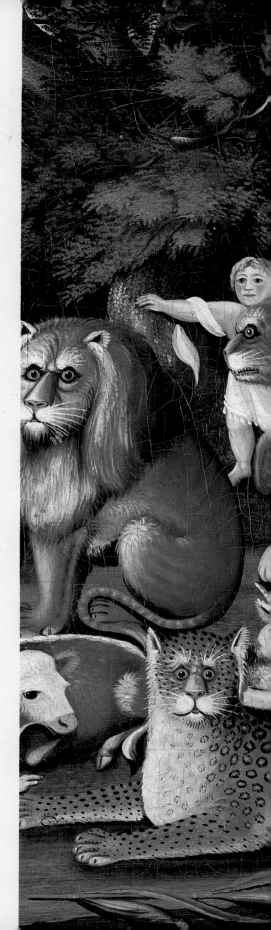

American Art

ANONYMOUS ARTIST
      American, late 17th century
      John Freake
      Mrs. Elizabeth Freake and Baby Mary
      about 1671–74
      American
      Oil on canvas
      42½ × 36¾ in. (107.9 × 93.4 cm) each
      Sarah C. Garver Fund, 1963.135 and
      Gift of Mr. and Mrs. Albert W. Rice,
      1963.134

These portraits of a wealthy Bostonian and his wife and daughter (the youngest of their eight children) are among the most important of the relatively small number that survive from the late seventeenth century in New England. A half-dozen portraits painted in Boston during the 1670s can be attributed to the same anonymous artist, who gave greater attention to costume than to the characterization of the individuals. The colonial painter's deliberate, decorative style shows his awareness of a tradition in British portraiture that derives ultimately from late sixteenth-century iconic representations of Elizabeth I.

Research on the sitters and technical examination of the portraits support a theory that the artist updated the Freakes' portraits in 1674, about three years after he first painted them. It was then that the baby was added and details in costume were changed, probably to reflect current fashion. Similar items appear in both the portraits and a household inventory taken in 1675 following John Freake's death: a signet ring, a black coat, and gloves were among his possessions. Also listed were a set of twelve chairs with turkey-worked upholstery (one of which Mrs. Freake is seated upon) and yards of lemon-colored silk that could well have been used to make the child's dress. While little is revealed of the sitters' personalities in these portraits, their personal effects do denote the social and economic status of a prominent merchant and attorney and his family.

—SES

THOMAS SMITH

  American, died about 1691
  Self-Portrait, about 1680
  Oil on canvas
  24¾ × 23¾ in. (62.9 × 60.4 cm)
  Museum purchase, 1948.19

This painting is the only seventeenth-century New England portrait by an identified artist and the earliest extant American self-portrait. Few details are known about Smith, who was recorded as a portrait painter in a contemporary account book at Harvard College. A group of about four portraits of Bostonians painted between 1675 and 1690 can be attributed to Smith on the basis of style. That he was a man of wealth is confirmed by his inventory of 1691, as well as by his refined attire in the present portrait. A reference to Smith as a mariner, which appears in his will of 1688, is supported by the naval battle depicted in the vista to the left, which includes ships flying British and Dutch flags.

Among indications that Smith was acquainted with northern European portraiture are the modeling of rounded forms in this painting—especially the figure—and the illusion of real space. The skull and the poem—which bears the artist's initials at its conclusion—comment on the mortality of man, a theme recalling seventeenth-century Dutch and British precedents.   —SES

JOHN SINGLETON COPLEY

American, 1738–1815
John Bours, about 1765–70
Oil on canvas
50¼ × 40⅛ in. (127.6 × 101.9 cm)
Museum purchase with funds from the
bequest of Mrs. Hester Newton Wetherell,
1908.7

In an era when portraiture was the primary subject of colonial painters in America, Copley set an unprecedented standard for conveying both the physical and the psychological presence of his sitters. One of five portraits by Copley in the Museum's collection, the characterization of John Bours (1734–1815) is striking for its informality. A respected citizen of Newport, Rhode Island, and a devoted member of that town's Trinity Church, Bours is portrayed as a man of quiet intelligence in an introspective, pensive moment. This intimate likeness is rendered convincingly with a rich array of textures: the soft, brown velvet suit and crisp, white cuffs; the hard sheen of the mahogany chair; and the freely brushed landscape vista.

Copley's artistic achievement is all the more extraordinary considering that the colonies offered no opportunities for formal training for native-born artists. Instead he had to glean what lessons he could from engravings of fashionable British portraits, through occasional correspondence with artists abroad, or from the canvases that he could see in America. Within a few years after completing the portrait of Bours, Copley left behind lucrative patronage in Boston and New York to pursue greater artistic ambitions as a history painter in Europe and England.   —SES

High Chest of Drawers
   1760–80
   American (Newport, Rhode Island)
   Mahogany, poplar, pine, chestnut,
   and maple
   H: 82 in. (208.3 cm) W: 39¾ in. (101.6 cm)
   D: 20½ in. (52.1 cm)
   Partial gift of the son and daughters
   of Rebecca Wilder White and partial
   museum purchase, 1986.36

The high chest of drawers—a form of furniture produced throughout much of the eighteenth century in North America—was used to store linens and clothing. This particular high chest bears the understated design and construction features associated with cabinetmakers in Newport, Rhode Island. The simple, almost prim, lines and diminutive scale are enhanced by ball-and-claw front feet and pad rear feet, by a carved shell on the apron of the case, and by a closed scroll bonnet surmounting twin raised panels fronting the scroll board.

From the mid-1750s until the Revolution, Newport developed into an important center for furniture production, rivaling even Boston in its number of craftsmen. During this period Newport—and especially the workshops of two Quaker families, the Townsends and the Goddards—became known for the consistency in style and superb craftsmanship of its furniture, which was made for the colony's mercantile elite and for export to other cities along the eastern seaboard and beyond. Comparison of Newport high chests with more highly carved and ornamented examples made in Boston, New York, and Philadelphia underscores the restrained elegance of pieces from the Rhode Island port.   —SES

PAUL REVERE II

American, 1735–1818
Paine Service, 1773
Silver
H: 13½ in. (34.2 cm) coffeepot; H: 6⅝ in.
(16.8 cm) teapot; H: 9⁵⁄₁₆ in. (24.5 cm)
tankard
Gift of Frances Thomas Paine and Eliza S.
Paine in memory of Frederick William
Paine; Gift of the Paine Charitable Trust;
Gift of Dr. and Mrs. George C. Lincoln in
memory of Fanny Chandler Lincoln; and
Gift of Richard K. Thorndike; 1937.55–58,
1959.105, 1963.338a–f, 1965.336, 1967.57

This service, commissioned by Dr. William
Paine of Worcester for his bride, Lois Orne,
is one of the highest achievements in design
and craftsmanship credited to any eighteenth-
century New England silversmith. As the
centerpieces for the service, the coffeepot and
teapot represent a full-blown expression of
the graceful, organic Rococo style that became
popular in the colonies in the 1750s. Typical
are the "double-bellied," gravity-defying
forms of the pots, their ornate spouts cast
with vigorous C-scrolls and acanthus leaves,
the reeded banding of their raised feet, their
pineapple finials, and the asymmetrical engraved cartouche representing the coat of arms
and crest of the Orne family. The forty-five
pieces of flat and hollow ware of the original
Paine service, not produced as a matching set,
together represent the largest single order
recorded in Revere's ledgers. The price he
charged for it—£74 for the silver and £34
for production and engraving—was a sum
affordable by only the wealthiest patrons.
Illustrated above is a selection of the thirty
pieces of the *Paine Service* now owned by
the Museum.   —SES

BENJAMIN WEST
        American, 1738–1820
        *Pharaoh and His Host Lost in the
        Red Sea*, 1792
        Oil on canvas
        37½ × 29¼ in. (97.1 × 76.2 cm)
        Museum purchase, 1960.18

West's career served as a model for many
American painters of his day who aspired
to go beyond portraiture to depict loftier
themes from history and religion. Growing
up in modest circumstances in Philadelphia,
West became, in 1759, one of the first American artists to study abroad, and within four
years he had settled permanently in London.
Despite increasing tensions between Britain
and the colonies, the tactful and talented
young American was appointed history
painter to the king in 1772.

Pharaoh and His Host Lost in the Red Sea
is an unfinished study that West conceived as
part of an ambitious cycle depicting "Revealed
Religion" for the private chapel of George III
at Windsor Castle. The sense of drama and
terror of this episode from the Old Testament
is heightened by the metaphoric use of light
and darkness, the emotionally charged figures,
and the swirling, chaotic composition. In the
upper left the powerful Moses extends his
rod against the Egyptians, whose pharaoh is
engulfed below by the Red Sea. The idealized
figures of the reprieved Israelites are embraced
by divine light and the protection of the angel
of God.   —SES

CHARLES WILLSON PEALE
American, 1741–1827
Charles Pettit, 1792
Oil on canvas
35⅞ × 27 in. (91.1 × 68.6 cm)
Museum purchase, 1919.121

Peale's spare, yet congenial, depiction of the Philadelphian Charles Pettit (1736–1806) projects a tone of composed intelligence and cultivation that befits both artist and sitter. Like Peale, Pettit fought in the Continental Army; later he served in Congress (from 1785 to 1787) and founded the Insurance Company of North America. A well-educated and well-connected lawyer and merchant, Pettit was also a member of the American Philosophical Society and a trustee of the University of Pennsylvania.

With his considerable energy, intellect, and personal generosity, Peale epitomized the self-taught Renaissance man during the dynamic years of early nationhood in America. After a brief career as a craftsman in a variety of trades in his native Maryland, he traveled in 1765 to London to study painting with Benjamin West. Following the Revolution Peale emerged as the leading painter of distinguished patrons in the Middle Atlantic states. The museum he opened in 1786 in Philadelphia exhibited his portraits of patriots and statesmen along with nature specimens he had collected and catalogued. Peale left a long legacy, as a number of his seventeen children carried on his interests in the arts and sciences throughout much of the nineteenth century.   —SES

EDWARD SAVAGE
American, 1761–1817
*Liberty in the Form of the Goddess
of Youth: Giving Support to the
Bald Eagle,* 1796
Stipple engraving on cream laid paper
24 7/16 × 15 ¾ in. (62 × 37.9 cm) plate
Gift of Mrs. Kingsmill Marrs, 1925.1045

Born in Princeton, Massachusetts, Savage was one of many artist-entrepreneurs of the early Federal period in America. He was the proprietor of a succession of galleries in Philadelphia, New York, and Boston, where he exhibited his own paintings and patriotic prints. In Philadelphia, on 11 June 1796, the artist published this reduced version of one of his canvases. Clad in flowing white draperies and a garland of spring flowers, the newly embodied goddess tramples the symbols of monarchy: a key, the medal and garter of a royal order, and a broken scepter. The eagle, symbol of the Republic, descends on shafts of light, to be nourished by Liberty. The flag of the union, topped by a liberty cap, is visible through the clouds of war, which spew lightning to drive the British fleet from Boston harbor.

The popularity of Savage's composition in its day is reflected by many printed copies. This image was even translated into needlework, as seen in an embroidery in the Museum's collection made in 1804 by sixteen-year-old Mary Green of Worcester (acc. no. 1963.86).   —DA

RALPH EARL

American, 1751–1801
Looking East from Denny Hill, 1800
Oil on canvas
45 ¾ × 79 ⅜ in. (116.2 × 201.6 cm)
Museum purchase, 1916.97

According to local tradition, Colonel Thomas Denny, Jr., commissioned Earl to paint this panoramic view of Worcester, Massachusetts, shortly after Denny had moved from his family's hilltop homestead in Leicester to a house he had built nearby. Apparently Denny wanted to take to his new home a memento of the commanding prospect he had enjoyed since childhood. Earl was a logical choice for this unusual commission, in part because he had also grown up in Leicester, and he undoubtedly knew the Denny family.

Following seven years (1778–85) in England, where he had studied with Benjamin West, Earl became a noted portrait painter of merchants and professionals in New York and New England, often setting his subjects against a landscape background of the region. He was one of the first American artists to raise landscape above the level of purely dec-orative or fanciful scenes and house portraiture. Contemporaries admired the accuracy of his view depicting two churches in the town of Worcester and the Boston Post Road meandering eastward through the rolling spread of cultivated fields. —SES

ANNA SANDERS
>   American, 1791–1860
>   *Sampler,* 1801
>   Silk thread on linen
>   16¹³⁄₁₆ × 12¹³⁄₁₆ in. (43.7 × 32.5 cm)
>   Gift of Mrs. J. Templeman Coolidge, 1963.4

Still retaining much of the vivid color of its silk threads, this sampler worked by ten-year-old Anna Sanders is one of three known from Warren, Rhode Island, each signed and dated by a young girl between 1793 and 1803. Related compositionally to samplers made in Providence and Newport, all three Warren examples depict a central motif of a Georgian-style house with raised steps, flanked by two trees; a group of conversing figures worked in profile—perhaps a family—stands at the bottom of the scene, which is enframed by striped columns supporting an arch. Genea-logical study of the families of the three girls in Warren reveals that they were taught by the same schoolmistress, who had moved to the town from Newport during the Revolution, her teaching career spanning a quarter century. It was probably she who passed along to her pupils the basic design of the samplers, perhaps by adapting motifs from print sources. The inscription Anna Sanders worked at the bottom includes an acrostic verse in which the first letter of each line spells out the young maker's name.   —SES

GILBERT STUART
American, 1755–1828
Mrs. Perez Morton, about 1802
Oil on canvas
29⅛ × 24⅛ in. (74 × 61.3 cm)
Gift of the grandchildren of
Joseph Tuckerman, 1899.2

Notwithstanding his questionable business practices—often overlooked by patrons because of his artistic genius—Stuart was the most inventive and influential portrait painter of the Federal era. Much of his success rested on his ability to convey through an unlabored, graceful style the dignity and character of his subjects, whether they were presidents or merchants.

Praised in literary circles as "The American Sappho," the Boston poet Sarah Wentworth Apthorp (Mrs. Perez Morton; 1759–1846) sat for Stuart for three portraits, of which this is by far the most dynamic. An unfinished sketch, the picture reflects Stuart's emphasis on features and expression. Close examination shows that he first painted Mrs. Morton's arms folded at her waist and then redrew them adjusting her mantilla in a seemingly spontaneous gesture. The sympathetic rapport between artist and sitter revealed in this vibrant, intimate likeness is documented in an exchange of poetic verse in which the painter and poet each extol the talents of the other.

—SES

CHARLES-BALTHAZAR-JULIEN FÉVRET DE SAINT-MÉMIN

French, 1770–1852 (active in
America, 1793–1814)
Thomas Jefferson, 1804
Charcoal and black, white, and gray chalk
drawing on cream wove paper prepared
with pink ground
23⅞ × 16¹⁵⁄₁₆ in. (60.7 × 42.9 cm) sheet
Museum purchase, 1954.82

An aristocrat who found refuge from the storms of the French Revolution in the United States, Saint-Mémin became an artist, pressing a former gentleman's pastime into a profession. From 1793 until his return to France in 1814, he traveled through the States and the newly acquired Louisiana territory, making profile portraits with the aid of a mechanical device called a *physiognotrace.* This machine allowed the artist to trace the sitter's profile with precision onto paper. Saint-Mémin sold his portraits as a package that included a life-size drawing, a miniature printing plate, and several impressions of the tiny prints, suitable for mounting in a locket or a small frame. President Jefferson sat for this portrait when he was sixty-one years of age and nearing the end of his first term in office. This image of the famous statesman and architect of the Declaration of Independence has become renowned as an accurate likeness. It has often been used by the federal government on postage stamps and savings bonds.   —DA

JOHN VANDERLYN

American, 1775–1852
Sampson Vryling Stoddard Wilder,
about 1808–12
Oil on canvas
36¼ × 28⅞ in. (92.1 × 73.3 cm)
Gift of Lawrence Alan Haines in memory of
his father, Wilder Haydn Haines, 1981.331

At a time when fellow Americans set their sights on working in London, Vanderlyn made the singular decision in 1796 to study art in Paris. His striking portrait of Sampson Wilder (1780–1865), a wealthy Massachusetts merchant, clearly reflects the lessons Vanderlyn absorbed from contact with the work of such great French masters of neoclassicism as Jacques-Louis David and Jean-Auguste-Dominique Ingres. The aloof, self-contained demeanor of the sitter; the strong contour of the figure's sleeve repeated in the curve of the chair; the understated palette of browns, grays, and greens; and the smooth surface of the painting, with few traces of brushwork—all are characteristic of the French neoclassical style of the early nineteenth century.

When Vanderlyn painted Wilder, both men were part of a small American community in Paris. Wilder returned to Bolton, Massachusetts, in 1812; twelve years later he hosted the Marquis de Lafayette during a tour of the United States honoring the general's role in the American Revolution. Wilder's portrait, then, stands as an emblem of the contemporary French taste as favored by both artist and sitter.   —SES

JAMES PEALE
>American, 1749–1831
>*Still Life,* 1825
>Oil on panel
>18½ × 26⁹⁄₁₆ in. (46.9 × 67.4 cm)
>Museum purchase, 1939.37

Members of an influential family of Philadelphia painters, James Peale and his nephew Raphaelle (1774–1825) have been credited with setting a standard in still-life painting that contributed to a broader taste for this subject among American patrons during the 1820s. James began his artistic career as a portrait and miniature painter under the tutelage of his older, influential brother Charles Willson Peale. In an effort to avoid competing with one another in a tight art market during the post-Revolution era, the brothers agreed to divide their work in portraiture: James focused on miniature painting, while Charles did larger oils on canvas. As James

faced failing eyesight during the 1810s, he turned from the detailed work of miniature portraits to larger still-life and landscape subjects. Remarkably, he was seventy-six years old when he painted this elegant arrangement of apples and grapes spilling out of a Chinese export-porcelain bowl. James clearly delighted in the variety of textures —from the smooth sheen of porcelain and mahogany to the cloudy moisture of the grapes and the serrated edges of their leaves. The illusion of reality is heightened by placement of the fruit at the edge of a tabletop as if to tempt the viewer to reach for it.   —SES

REMBRANDT PEALE
  American, 1778–1860
  George Washington, 1827
  Lithograph on chine collé
  19⅛ × 15⅝ in. (48.7 × 39 cm) image
  The Charles E. Goodspeed Collection,
  1910.48.3546

In 1795, when President Washington sat for Charles Willson Peale, the artist's young son Rembrandt was allowed to paint his own portrait of the statesman. Thirty years later Rembrandt Peale returned to the subject, producing a series of idealized paintings and prints calculated to appeal to a nationalist cult fascinated by the heroic myth surrounding Washington. This lithograph, the most famous of the images, combined the painter's own recollections with elements from famed portraits by his father and by Gilbert Stuart.

One of the first American artists to use lithography, Peale drew his original portrait directly on the printing surface. The image was then printed by William S. and John B. Pendleton, Peale's former students, who ran one of America's most important early lithographic workshops in Boston. Such prints disseminated Peale's art to a broad audience, helping to publicize his paintings and increase his reputation. In this version of the famous portrait, the illusionistic stonework was decorated with a carved keystone representing the mask of Zeus, supreme ruler of the ancient gods. The stonework also includes a garland of oak leaves, Zeus's symbol, and the carved legend PATRIAE PATER (father of the country). Thus, physically and symbolically isolated from the everyday world, Washington was presented more as a deified hero than a historical personage.   —DA

SAMUEL F. B. MORSE
American, 1791–1872
The Chapel of the Virgin at Subiaco, 1830
Oil on canvas
29¹⁵⁄₁₆ × 37 in. (76 × 94 cm)
Bequest of Stephen Salisbury III, 1907.35

Best known today for inventions like the tele-
graph, Morse early had aspirations of becoming a painter and spent five years (1811–15)
in London studying art. Despite unsuccessful
efforts to encourage an appreciation of history
painting among patrons in New York, Morse
rose to prominence as an artist in the 1820s
and 1830s.

On a second trip to Europe in April 1830,
Morse encountered in Rome a fellow American, Stephen Salisbury II of Worcester, who
commissioned a painting. This view of a way-
side chapel in the Sabine Mountains on the
road to Subiaco, sketched during an excur-
sion, was painted in Morse's Rome studio.
The Museum now owns not only the finished
work but also two preparatory oil sketches—
one depicting the shrine and surrounding
landscape (acc. no. 1941.16), another of the
shepherds and flock (acc. no. 1991.15). Comparison of the final composition and the landscape study shows that Morse transformed
the naturalistic palette and even quality of
noonday light in the study to create a more
dramatic mood: the finished painting is distinctive for its brilliant, artificial palette and
strong, late-afternoon light.   —SES

EDWARD HICKS

American, 1780–1849
The Peaceable Kingdom, about 1833
Oil on canvas
17½ × 23¹¹⁄₁₆ in. (44.5 × 60.2 cm)
Museum purchase, 1934.65

Trained as a sign, coach, and ornamental painter, Hicks painted over a hundred versions of his now-famous *Peaceable Kingdom* between 1820 and his death. His artistic endeavors provided modest support for his activities as a Quaker preacher in Bucks County, Pennsylvania. The theme of this painting, drawn from chapter 11 of Isaiah, was undoubtedly attractive to Hicks and fellow Quakers not only for its appealing imagery but also for its message of peace: "The wolf also shall dwell with the lamb, and the leopard shall lie down with the kid, and the calf and the young lion and fatling together; and a little child shall lead them." Into many versions, including the Worcester painting, Hicks incorporated a vignette of William Penn's treaty with the Indians, an image he adapted from a popular painting by Benjamin West. Hicks may have viewed parallels in the two parts of the composition, inasmuch as Penn, who had introduced Quakerism into Pennsylvania, had also brought about a measure of the peaceable kingdom on earth.   —SES

THOMAS COLE
   American (born in England), 1801–48
   View on the Arno, near Florence, 1837
   Oil on canvas
   33 ¼ × 53 ¼ in. (84.5 × 135.3 cm)
   Gift of Martha Esty Michie, 1991.179

Cole rose to prominence in the late 1820s as America's first important landscape painter. By enriching his compositions with human activity that conveys messages of moral or historical import, he raised the status of landscape painting in this country above mere topographical rendering. Essentially self-taught, but well aware of the European landscape tradition, he first traveled to Europe in June 1829 to study the old masters firsthand. In contrast to the wildness of American scenery, which he painted in New York's Catskill Mountains, the overgrown ruins and ancient architecture of Italy spoke eloquently to him about the rise and fall of great civilizations.

Of all the Italian cities Cole visited, Florence—where he spent several months in 1831 and 1832—was his favorite. During subsequent years he composed several major oils from sketches he had made along the Arno River, including four versions of this view from the Florence house of the Bostonian Horace Gray. The present canvas, originally owned by Gray, shows the meanders of the Arno flanked by crenellated walls and towers, while fanciful figures carry on their daily activities. For Cole it was an idyllic vision celebrating the harmonious coexistence of man's cultural achievements and the glory of nature.   —SES

ELIZA GOODRIDGE
  American, 1798–1882
  Stephen Salisbury III, 1838
  Watercolor on ivory housed in a leather
  case with velvet and ormolu mats
  4⅛ × 3 1/16 in. (10.5 × 7.8 cm)
  Gift of Stephen Salisbury III, 1901.39

American portrait miniatures find their ante-
cedents in sixteenth-century England during
the reign of Henry VIII. This intimate art
form enjoyed its heyday in America from
about 1760 to 1850, when photography over-
took miniature painting as a quicker, less expensive means of portraiture. Until the 1830s
most small-scale portraits painted on thin,
oval slices of ivory were worn as keepsakes
in metal lockets. During the 1820s and 1830s
a growing percentage of miniatures were
painted on slightly larger pieces of ivory,
often rectangular in format and framed in
hinged leather cases that could be displayed
on tabletops.

It was about this time that a number of
women—like Eliza Goodridge and her sister
Sarah (1788–1853), both born in Templeton,
Massachusetts, in Worcester County—became
recognized miniature painters. When Eliza
painted young Stephen Salisbury III (1835–
1905) pretending to drive a carriage, she was
staying in Worcester at the home of family
friends, where her patrons came to sit for
their portraits. Salisbury founded the Worcester Art Museum in 1896, and his gifts and
bequests of painting, sculpture, furniture,
miniatures, and daguerreotypes form an important nucleus of the American collections.

—SES

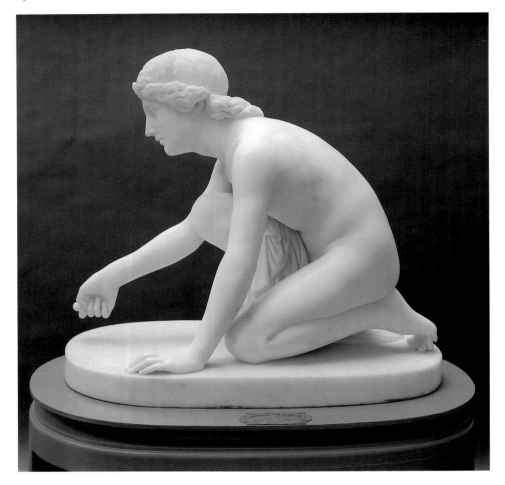

THOMAS CRAWFORD
        American, 1813–57
        Boy Playing Marbles, 1853
        Marble
        H: 27¾ in. (71.5 cm) W: 15⅝ in. (39.5 cm)
        L: 30¹⁵⁄₁₆ in. (78.5 cm)
        Bequest of Stephen Salisbury III, 1906.116

In 1853, on one of his European tours, Stephen Salisbury II (1798–1884)—father of the Museum's founder—visited the American neoclassical sculptor Thomas Crawford at his studio in Rome. Crawford, who had lived in Rome for almost twenty years, welcomed many American tourists. His reputation in the United States, and especially in New England, was greatly enhanced by the exhibition in Boston in 1844 of his sculpture *Orpheus,* which had been inspired by the renowned *Apollo Belvedere,* a centerpiece of the Vatican's rich collections of ancient art.

During his stay in Rome, Salisbury selected this subject from the many plaster maquettes (models) he saw in Crawford's studio. With the help of his studio assistants who carved the piece in marble, Crawford transformed the prosaic activity of a boy shooting marbles into a graceful, elegant composition. The supple, curving silhouette of the human form is enhanced by the sensuous surfaces of the polished marble. The classical details of the draped garment and disheveled hair tamed by a headband clearly indicate that Crawford drew inspiration from ancient sources.

—SES

Salisbury House, Worcester, Massachusetts
about 1857
American
Daguerreotype
6½ × 8½ in. (16.5 × 21.6 cm)
Bequest of Stephen Salisbury III, 1907.601

Taken over 130 years ago, this rare whole-plate daguerreotype depicts a Classical Revival home designed by the Worcester architect-builder Elias Carter (1781–1864). Although the barn, grounds, and orchard no longer exist, the house, built in 1838 for Stephen Salisbury II (1798–1884)—father of the Museum's founder—still stands on present-day Harvard Street in Worcester. With wood construction simulating stonework and a porch supported by Doric columns, the house is an imposing example of the latest architectural taste of its day.

This landscape view represents the less common use of a popular medium employed primarily for taking studio portraits in the mid-nineteenth century. The photographic process, which produced a direct-positive image from nature by optical and chemical means on a sensitized silvered plate, was introduced to the United States by Samuel F. B. Morse and Dr. John W. Draper, professors at the University of the City of New York, soon after the French artist Louis Jacques Mandé Daguerre announced his invention to the world in 1839.　　　　　　　　　　—SBJ

JAMES ABBOTT MCNEILL WHISTLER
American, 1834–1903
Sketch for *Rose and Silver: La Princesse du Pays de la Porcelaine,* 1863–64
Oil on fiberboard
24⅛ × 13⅜ in. (61.5 × 34 cm)
Theodore T. and Mary G. Ellis Collection, 1940.56

An eccentric personality whose innovative ideas about art often placed him at odds with critics of his day, Whistler has proved to be one of the most influential artists of the late nineteenth century. Several of his paintings of the 1860s reflect his interest in Chinese and Japanese arts. Revealing a preference for asymmetrical compositions with brightly patterned surfaces, Whistler incorporated such exotic props as screens, woodblock prints, and ceramics in portraits of European women posed in Oriental costumes. Worcester's painting is a preparatory study for a portrait of Christine Spartali, whose father served as Greek consul-general in London while Whistler was there. This fluidly brushed sketch blocks out the general arrangement and color scheme of the more detailed finished work. The final portrait, which the consul-general refused to buy, became, about a decade after its completion, a focal point in the dining room of Whistler's first significant patron, Frederick Leyland. Whistler transformed the room (now housed at the Freer Gallery of Art, Washington, D.C.) into a luxuriant setting for Leyland's collection of blue-and-white porcelain, thus giving rise to the title of the larger portrait and this sketch.   —SES

MATHEW B. BRADY
American, 1823–96
General Robert E. Lee and Staff, 1865
Albumen print
8½ × 7⁷⁄₁₆ in. (21.5 × 17.9 cm)
Sarah C. Garver Fund, 1988.155

This photograph is one of the most celebrated images produced by Brady, who established his reputation in the 1850s as the preeminent portraitist in New York and Washington, D.C. In the aftermath of the Civil War, Brady sought out General Robert E. Lee, who had returned to the Confederate capital at Richmond, Virginia, after his surrender to General Ulysses S. Grant at Appomattox Court House on April 9, 1865. At the photographer's request General Lee reluctantly put on his uniform and posed at the back of his residence with his son, General George Washington Custis Lee (left), and his chief of staff, Colonel Walter H. Taylor (right). The image conveys the pathos of defeat for the Confederacy and for Lee personally. For Brady, who had been present at the first battle of the Civil War at Bull Run, this portrait completed his photographic coverage of the conflict. —SBJ

ALBERT BIERSTADT
American (born in Germany), 1830–1902
Yosemite Falls, about 1865–70
Oil on canvas
36 × 26⅛ in. (91.4 × 66.4 cm)
Gift from the estate of Mrs. William H.
Sawyer, 1954.66

Bierstadt's reputation was firmly established in the early 1860s through paintings celebrating natural wonders of the American West that expeditions had begun to survey only a decade before. The grandeur of the Rockies and the Sierra Nevada, acclaimed in newspapers and popular literature back East, aroused national pride in these newfound natural splendors rivaling Europe's great Alps in the public's imagination. During his second trip west in 1863, Bierstadt visited Yosemite Valley, making oil sketches and drawings that would serve as studies for finished paintings he would compose in his New York studio. In contrast to canvases that suggest the expansiveness of the western landscape in monumental scale, the Museum's painting of Yosemite Falls is modest in its dimensions. Dramatic interest is created through the interplay of atmospheric effects: the spray from the falls above and the glassy reflections in the still water below.   —SES

GEORGE INNESS
American, 1825–94
The Alban Hills, 1873
Oil on canvas
30 × 45 in. (76.2 × 144.3 cm)
Gift from the Lucius J. Knowles Art Fund
and museum purchase, 1906.1

Essentially self-taught, Inness benefited from study of the old masters and from extensive European travel. In Paris during the early 1850s, he was influenced also by French Barbizon painters, whose informal compositions rendered with bright, naturalistic color were often painted directly from nature rather than executed in the studio in the traditional manner. As his career progressed, Inness revealed an increasing interest in effusive light and color, expressive brushwork, and suppression of detail to create mood.

One of six landscapes by Inness in the Museum's collection, *The Alban Hills* was painted during his second European trip (1870–75), which he spent principally in Italy. He painted these scenic hills south of Rome many times, undoubtedly knowing that the subject would appeal to potential patrons. Yet specific details of the shepherds, their sheep, and rock formations are rendered in a manner then considered cursory, as Inness focused instead on the overall quality of light and color and the expansiveness of the vista to suggest a feeling of reverence for the nature before him. —SES

WINSLOW HOMER
American, 1836–1910
Boys and Kitten, 1873
Watercolor and gouache over graphite
on cream wove paper
9⅝ × 13⅝ in. (24.4 × 34.6 cm) sheet
Museum purchase, Sustaining
Membership Fund, 1911.1

Trained in lithography and wood engraving, Homer embarked on a career as an illustrator for *Harper's Weekly* during the Civil War. A trip to France in 1866 and 1867 exposed him to the early work of the Impressionists and sparked his interest in light and color. Homer's first serious use of watercolor may have been precipitated by an important exhibition in New York early in 1873. It was during that summer in Gloucester, Massachusetts, that the artist produced a series of small watercolors involving the theme of children playing.

The decorative flatness and sharp contrasts of light and shade in Homer's works of this period relate to his ongoing career as a magazine illustrator. In *Boys and Kitten* liberal application of white gouache, or opaque watercolor, creates dazzling highlights and helps to emphasize the structure of the composition. Employing saturated, opaque color, rather than the transparent washes that were to predominate in his later works, Homer worked from dark to light as he did in oil painting. Holding watercolors in as high esteem as oils, Homer accorded his subjects a monumentality that raised the level of prestige for that medium.   —AD

WINSLOW HOMER
American, 1836–1910
The Gale, 1883–93
Oil on canvas
30¼ × 48⁵⁄₁₆ in. (76.8 × 122.7 cm)
Museum purchase, 1916.48

Early in his career, in the 1870s, Homer was widely admired for depictions of the Civil War and for idyllic scenes of rural America. The tenor of his work changed decisively, however, during a two-year stay (1881–83) in the English village of Tynemouth on the coast of the North Sea. In both watercolor and oil Homer now focused on the fisherfolk who braved the dangerous sea to earn their spare livelihood. The subject of a robust fisherwoman facing the elements with her baby strapped to her back fits squarely within this theme of man's struggle against natural forces.

The present work was first painted in Tynemouth and exhibited in 1883 as *The Coming Away of the Gale* at the National Academy of Design in New York City. Probably because the original composition incurred unfavorable criticism, Homer kept it for nearly a decade at his studio in Prout's Neck, Maine, before reworking the canvas. He painted out a pavilion and dory at the left, adding the rocks and ocean spray in their place. By the time *The Gale* was shown at the 1893 World's Fair in Chicago, receiving high acclaim, Homer's reputation as one of America's foremost artists was secure.   —SES

JOHN SINGER SARGENT
American (born in Italy), 1856–1925
Venetian Water Carriers, 1880–82
Oil on canvas
25⅜ × 27¾ in. (64.4 × 70.6 cm)
Museum purchase, 1911.30

Not yet the famous portrait painter and muralist he would become in the 1890s, the young, cosmopolitan Sargent painted between 1880 and 1882 a remarkable group of figure compositions inspired by two extended visits to Venice during those years. Rather than focusing on the famous picturesque monuments and canals of this luminous city, Sargent portrayed predominantly working-class women within the dark, mysterious enclosed spaces of unadorned halls, courtyards, and back streets. These candid scenes of ordinary Venetian life, which went unappreciated by critics initially, reflect a masterful talent by an artist then only in his mid-twenties. From studying the work of such seventeenth-century masters as Diego Velázquez and Frans Hals, Sargent had learned important lessons that reverberate in his muted palette of gray, black, and brown,

highlighted by touches of red and bright white, and the broad, decisive application of brushstrokes to define form, texture, and light.

Although seemingly informal, if not spontaneous, in both design and execution, *Venetian Water Carriers* is actually carefully conceived. Within a composition centered around rectangular forms (the door and its frame, the well and its base), Sargent subtly balanced the figure of the woman straining to carry a pail with the tilt of the door hanging off its hinges. With equal mastery he varied his technique, using exacting strokes of the brush, fluidly applied, to define individual pavement stones and building up rough layers of color to simulate the peeling plaster wall.   —SES

JOHN SINGER SARGENT
American (born in Italy), 1856–1925
Muddy Alligators, 1917
Watercolor over graphite on off-white
wove paper
13⁹⁄₁₆ × 20⅞ in. (35.5 × 53 cm) sheet
Museum purchase, Sustaining
Membership Fund, 1917.86

Sargent was the foremost portraitist in London and the United States at the turn of the century, but by 1910 he undertook portraiture only rarely. During the preceding decade watercolor had become an important aspect of his production, and he frequently looked to this medium as a means for personal expression, a respite from the constraints of mural commissions and portrait painting. *Muddy Alligators* seems to have been such a diversion, painted to offset the frustration of a work in progress: a portrait of John D. Rockefeller at his winter home in Ormond Beach, Florida.

A seemingly unlikely subject for a fashionable painter, alligators caked with mud nevertheless presented a pictorial challenge that recurs in Sargent's oeuvre: the depiction of light and shadow on sun-drenched forms. This menacing mass of serpentine creatures evoked intriguing possibilities of surface and texture, to which the artist brought to bear the resources of his bravura technique. A number of preparatory sketches exist for *Muddy Alligators*: four graphite drawings, all of which the Worcester Art Museum owns, and two watercolors (in the Metropolitan Museum of Art, New York; and the Ormond Family Collection). This finished watercolor reveals a diversity of means: scratching into the paper to denote teeth, applying wax resist to suggest rough textures, and laying on broad brushstrokes to delineate tree trunks.

—AD

THOMAS EAKINS
>American, 1844–1916
>*Study of the Head of Samuel David Gross,*
>1875
>Oil on canvas
>24 1/16 × 18 3/16 in. (61.1 × 46.2 cm)
>Museum purchase, 1929.124

In 1875 the young Eakins searched for a theme that would represent him well at the nation's Centennial exhibition in his native Philadelphia. The subject he chose was an ambitious one, far from the safe, traditional history tableau a less adventuresome artist would have submitted for such an important occasion. Painted on a monumental scale, the finished composition shows an operation and medical demonstration performed by the world-famous surgeon Samuel David Gross at Philadelphia's Jefferson Medical College. *The Gross Clinic* (acquired by the college in 1878 and still displayed there) relates directly to Eakins's own experience as an art student who had witnessed many medical procedures in an effort to understand the intricacies of human anatomy.

Following his typical working method, Eakins painted several preparatory studies for his masterpiece, in which the surgeon, holding a blood-covered scalpel, stands over the patient in the center of an amphitheater full of spectators. For Worcester's sketch Eakins used a palette knife to capture the essential volumes of the head; the dramatic splash of light on the forehead conveys the genius he saw in the heroic image of Dr. Gross.   —SES

EADWEARD MUYBRIDGE

American (born in England), 1830–1904
Jumping a hurdle; saddle; bay horse Daisy
Plate 640 of *Animal Locomotion*, 1887
Collotype
10 × 12 1/16 in. (25.4 × 30.6 cm)
Gift of John Rogers, 1973.163

Muybridge gained fame in 1878 by successfully photographing former Governor Leland Stanford's racehorse, Sallie Gardner, galloping before cameras in Palo Alto, California. He went to Philadelphia five years later on the recommendation of the painter Thomas Eakins, who shared his enthusiasm for photographing and studying the motion of humans and animals. Commissioned by the University of Pennsylvania to undertake further studies, Muybridge produced 781 photolithographic prints for his pioneering work *Animal Locomotion*. The publication was intended to provide well-defined pictures of the human figure and animals from which artists could understand and delineate with exactitude poses not previously seen by the naked eye.

In this series of consecutive frames, a bay horse and her rider proceed down a track and over a hurdle before a row of twenty cameras placed at a right angle to the mare's path. To make the exposures the photographer employed electromagnetic shutters that fired sequentially through a clock-driven electrical device.   —SBJ

MARY CASSATT
American, 1844–1926
The Letter, 1890–91
Drypoint and aquatint on cream laid paper
13⁹⁄₁₆ × 8¹⁵⁄₁₆ in. (34.5 × 22.7 cm) plate
Bequest of Mrs. Kingsmill Marrs, 1926.205

Although best known as a painter, Cassatt was also one of the pioneering color printmakers of the late nineteenth century. An American living in Paris, she enjoyed an exceptionally close relationship with the French Impressionists. Working in the circle of Edgar Degas and Camille Pissarro, she adopted their innovative attitude toward technique in the graphic arts, experimenting with effects of light, atmosphere, and texture. In the months following a landmark exhibition of Japanese color woodcuts in Paris in 1890, Cassatt was inspired to make a series of ten drypoints colored with aquatint. Adapting the *ukiyo-e* theme of woman's daily routine to one descriptive of the modern-day French woman, she crafted such scenes as a mother caring for her child, a young woman at her toilette, another trying on a dress, and this letter writer sealing an envelope. As seen here in the deft handling of drypoint line and the careful balance of large areas of tone with fine patterning, the artist translated the simplified design and muted palette of Japanese prints into the medium of intaglio (processes that involve cutting into a metal printing surface). Cassatt then collaborated with a master printer to produce an edition of twenty-five impressions of each plate in this set, varying every impression to achieve the novel effects prized by collectors of Japanese art.   —AD

MARY CASSATT
  American, 1844–1926
  Reine Lefebvre Holding a Nude Baby, 1902
  Oil on canvas
  26¹³/₁₆ × 22⁹/₁₆ in. (66.5 × 57.3 cm)
  Museum purchase, 1909.15

The daughter of a prosperous, socially prominent Pittsburgh family, Cassatt resolved about
1860 to become an artist. After traveling in
Europe to study the old masters, she settled
in Paris, where in 1877 she was invited by
Edgar Degas to join the French Impressionists. Cassatt exhibited several times with the
group between 1879 and 1886, thereby becoming the only American so intimately
associated with these radical artists.

  While landscapes and scenes of the city and
its cafés and theaters were favored by many of
her male colleagues, Cassatt focused on intimate, domestic subjects, such as the theme of
mother and child that she repeated throughout her career. By 1902 the artist had lived
for almost a decade in the village of Mesnil-
Theribus (about fifty miles northwest of
Paris), where she often had neighbors pose
for her, as they seemed more at ease than
professional models. The young mother in
Worcester's painting sat for Cassatt many
times in 1902 and 1903, appearing in several
preparatory sketches done in both oil and
pastel. This final version reveals the characteristic solid forms and design that had emerged
in Cassatt's work in the 1890s, when she was
first influenced by the strong patterns and
contours in Japanese prints.   —SES

JOHN LA FARGE

American, 1835–1910
Peacock Window, 1892–1908
Stained glass
40 × 20 in. (101.5 × 50.7 cm)
Museum purchase, 1909.11

At the time when America was emerging as a force in the international art world, La Farge stood out as a versatile artist and designer working in a variety of media. His extraordinary range as a student of world culture and as a muralist, painter, and designer led to his collaboration with leading American architects. Characteristically, when he first turned his attention to stained glass in the late 1870s, he showed remarkable stylistic and technical freedom in this difficult medium.

The *Peacock Window,* which simulates the vibrant coloration of a magnificent, exotic bird, represents La Farge's final effort in fused, or *cloisonné,* glass. Begun in 1892 as one of a pair of windows for the Washington, D.C., home of John Hay, the piece was not presented to the client, apparently because of difficulties encountered in the successive firings required to fuse layers of glass. Instead La Farge provided Hay with a window of the same design made of more conventional leaded opalescent glass (now at Museum Stuck-Villa in Munich). Several years later the artist returned to his original concept to produce this window.   —SES

MAURICE BRAZIL PRENDERGAST
American, 1858–1924
Low Tide, Beachmont, about 1902–4
Watercolor over graphite and charcoal on
off-white wove paper
19¼ × 22⅛ in. (48.8 × 56.2 cm) sheet
Museum purchase, 1941.34

A prolific painter who favored the watercolor medium during most of his career, Prendergast worked in Boston as a commercial artist before training at the Académie Julian and the Atelier Colarossi in Paris from 1891 to 1894. Upon his return to Boston, he exhibited watercolors of coastal scenes, which he had made both in Brittany and in Massachusetts. The seaside was to be a fertile source for Prendergast's art for the rest of his life. Drawn to the populated urban beaches north of Boston, such as Revere Beach and Beachmont, he used working-class promenaders dressed in finery to engage issues of class and fashion. In this he was an heir to French avant-garde painting of the spectacle of modern life.

Low Tide, Beachmont reverses the relative importance of figure and setting seen in Prendergast's earlier works: here the people, arranged in rows, predominate. While they are rendered decoratively with little sense of roundness of form, the harbor scene is more lifelike, full of light, atmosphere, and movement. In his daring treatment of the human form, the artist drew on a variety of sources, including Post-Impressionism and folk art.

—AD

FRANK BENSON
American, 1862–1951
Portrait of My Daughters, 1907
Oil on canvas
26 × 36⅛ in. (66 × 91.7 cm)
Museum purchase, 1908.4

Some fifteen years after its inception in France during the 1870s, Impressionism gained widespread public recognition in America and remained enormously popular well into the 1920s. As a founding member in 1897 of The Ten American Painters, a group that included this country's most talented Impressionists, Benson enjoyed considerable national stature. His reputation also rested firm as a leader of the so-called Boston School, a circle of regional painters specializing in figural subjects posed in idealized interiors and outdoor settings.

Benson's wife, three daughters, and son were his favorite subjects, and the artist's affection for his family pervades the likenesses he made of them. In this canvas (left to right) Elizabeth, Sylvia, and Eleanor are captured in quiet repose against a sun-filled vista at Wooster Farm, which Benson purchased in 1901 as a summer place on North Haven, an island off the coast of Maine in Penobscot Bay. Such idyllic compositions allowed the artist to combine an interest in the figure and a preference for plein air, or outdoor, painting. Although the style of this oil derives from the bright, high-keyed palette and energetic brushwork of the French Impressionists, the solidity of the figures reflects the lingering influence of Benson's early training with academic painters.

—SES

ALFRED STIEGLITZ
American, 1864–1946
The Steerage, 1907
Photogravure
13⅛ × 10⁷⁄₁₆ in. (33.3 × 26.5 cm)
Gift of Mr. and Mrs. Hall James Peterson,
1978.76

The dominant force in the Photo-Secession group he founded, Stieglitz exerted profound influence on the development of American creative photography in the twentieth century. His efforts to establish this medium as a fine art are perhaps best remembered through his first magazine, *Camera Work,* which appeared from 1903 to 1917. This large-format photogravure was produced by a photochemical printing process for the art magazine *291,* published by Stieglitz in 1915 and 1916. The magazine was named after his New York gallery at 291 Fifth Avenue, where he promoted modern art—primarily photography, painting, and sculpture.

Stieglitz regarded *The Steerage* as one of his best works. Using a hand-held four-by-five-inch camera, he captured on an eastbound Atlantic crossing this poignant picture of steerage passengers who, having been rejected by United States immigration officials, were being sent back to Europe. Attracted to the abstract compositional elements of the scene, Stieglitz recalled: "I saw shapes related to one another—a picture of shapes, and underlying it, a new vision that held me: simple people; the feeling of the ship, ocean, sky. . . ."   —SBJ

ARTHUR B. DAVIES
   American, 1862–1928
   Sleep Lies Perfect in Them, 1908
   Oil on canvas
   18⅛ × 40⁵⁄₁₆ in. (46 × 101.7 cm)
   Gift of Cornelius N. Bliss, 1941.7

The eclectic art of Davies drew upon disparate sources—the romantic, poetic idealism of the late nineteenth century as well as the radical movements leading toward abstract art that arose in the first two decades of this century. A visible leader in the New York art scene in the 1910s, Davies was a mercurial personality who kept his personal life secretive: he had two separate families who remained unknown to each other until after his death.

Much of Davies's work in painting, prints, and watercolors is about mood rather than realistic representation. The content of *Sleep Lies Perfect in Them,* for example—nude or classically garbed female figures posed silently within a landscape setting—is remote from real life and is rendered in a decorative style. A major work from the artist's early maturity, its subject is typical, as is its evocation of goddesses from ancient mythology. Davies created an otherworldly idyll of slumber using subtle visual means: set within a horizontal expanse and painted in a quiet, muted palette, the contours of the recumbent figures echo the silhouette of distant mountains.   —SES

CHILDE HASSAM
  American, 1859–1935
  The Breakfast Room, Winter Morning,
  1911
  Oil on canvas
  25⅛ × 30⅛ in. (63.8 × 76.5 cm)
  Museum purchase, 1911.29

The idealized representation of a modern woman of leisure captured during an introspective moment was a popular subject for American artists at the turn of the century. About 1910 Hassam, one of America's foremost Impressionists, began the *New York Window* series, a group of paintings depicting a contemplative woman posed before a curtained window. In *The Breakfast Room* the form of the faceless subject is one of several elements—including the seemingly mundane silhouette of the window, the vase of flowers, and the bowl of fruit—that the artist used to balance his asymmetrical composition. Clearly, Hassam delighted in differentiating the visual effects of light on various textures, such as the sheer curtain, the gossamer fabric of the sitter's dress, the reflective surface of the tabletop, and the sparkling transparency of the glass vase.

—SES

CHARLES SHEELER
American, 1883–1965
Zinnia and Nasturtium Leaves, 1915
Gelatin silver print
9⅝ × 7¹¹⁄₁₆ in. (24.4 × 19.6 cm)
Anonymous gift, 1977.144

Having studied at the Pennsylvania Academy of the Fine Arts and under the Impressionist William Merritt Chase in New York, Sheeler took up architectural photography in 1912 as a means of supporting his painting. As both painter and photographer he focused on the sense of structure and form of his subjects, whether they were still lifes, buildings, interiors, machinery, or industrial environments. *Zinnia and Nasturtium Leaves*—one of eight photographs by Sheeler in the Museum's collection—emphasizes this structural character through the assertive forms of the stems, leaves, and flower, anchored by a round bowl.

The artist, who took this matter-of-fact still life at a time when the soft-focus, idyllic imagery of pictorialism dominated American photography, once stated: "I have come to value photography more and more for those things which it alone can accomplish, rather than to discredit it for the things which can only be achieved through another medium."

—SBJ

CHARLES SHEELER
American, 1883–1965
City Interior, 1936
Aqueous adhesive and oil on
composition board
22⅛ × 26⅞ in. (56.2 × 68.4 cm)
Museum purchase in memory of Jonathan
and Elizabeth M. Sawyer, 1937.3

In October 1927, just prior to the introduction
of the Model A, Sheeler was commissioned
to photograph Ford Motor Company's River
Rouge plant near Dearborn, Michigan. By
then a noted commercial photographer and
a moderately successful painter, he spent six
weeks making photographs to be published
in advertisements for Ford's innovative prod-
ucts. These images would be exhibited also
as fine-art photography, and many of them
served as sources for a group of paintings,
including Worcester's *City Interior,* that
Sheeler executed during the mid-1930s.

As his River Rouge photographs and
paintings attest, Sheeler was impressed
with the magnitude of the factory complex
as well as with its design and technology.
City Interior—developed from a gouache
study now in the Museum's collection (acc.
no. 1977.143)—depicts, on the left, a sinter-
ing (heating) plant and, on the right, a blast
furnace where slag was channeled through
a pipe into buggies to be carted away. Emphasizing the visual rhythms created by the
web of pipes and railroad tracks and by the
repeated rectilinear elements of windows
and steel girders, Sheeler imbued the architecture with a lively, organic energy. Giving
no hint of the grime or pollution in factories, the painting idealizes the automotive
industry and its role in the progress of
technology.   —SES

GEORGE BELLOWS
American, 1882–1925
The White Horse, 1922
Oil on canvas
34⅛ × 44⅟₁₆ in. (86.7 × 111.9 cm)
Museum purchase, 1929.109

An artist who focused on democratic subject matter in modern American life, Bellows was one of the most talented realists working in the first quarter of this century. While he is best remembered for robust scenes of New York City—from gritty construction sites and congested tenements to boys skinny dipping off docks and sprawling prizefighters locked in combat—he was also an accomplished painter of portraits and landscapes. Personally energetic and athletic, Bellows conveyed a physical directness in his canvases through rich application of paint and expressive use of color and light.

The White Horse was painted in November 1922, about two years before Bellows's tragic death from appendicitis at age forty-two. It depicts a farm near Woodstock, New York, an artist's colony in the Catskills where Bellows and his family had summered and where he had just built a house and studio. The vivid autumnal color and the dramatic contrast of strong light and deep shadows created by the passing of heavy clouds lend an air of mystery and dynamism to an otherwise ordinary rural scene.   —SES

EDWARD WESTON
American, 1886–1958
In a Glendale Studio, 1923
Platinum print
6 ¹⁄₁₆ × 8 ⁷⁄₁₆ in. (15.3 × 21.5 cm)
Gift of William H. and Saundra B. Lane,
1981.339

Weston, one of photography's modern masters, pursued a productive career that bridged two styles: the soft-focus pictorialism of the 1910s and the 1920s and the sharp-focus realism that became an established art form in the 1930s. Inspired by Japanese aesthetics, Weston balanced in this image the pine bough in a ceramic jar with the nude figure against a paneled setting. To heighten the expressive quality he exploited the subtle tonal gradations of the platinum process.

Weston's future shift to hard-edge imagery is predicted here in the ordered compositional structure of the scene. He had already produced his first important sharp-focus photographs at the Armco steel mill in Ohio and would soon go to Mexico to evaluate and redirect his work. There he evolved a new vision by emphasizing physical properties—form, substance, and texture. From the mid-1920s until the end of his life, Weston revealed the essence of his subjects through straightforward photographs of shells, vegetables, nudes, and landscapes.   —SBJ

DIEGO RIVERA

Mexican, 1886–1957
Mother and Child, 1927
Graphite drawing on cream laid paper
24¾ × 18⅝ (62.8 × 47.3 cm) sheet
Museum purchase, 1928.4

The most famous Mexican painter of his age, Rivera was a pioneer in the mural revival of the mid-twentieth century. After a precocious childhood he was sent to study in Europe in 1907 with the support of the governor of Veracruz. For fourteen years he lived in Spain and in Paris, experimenting with Cubism, Surrealism, and other radical styles. Although he never became devoted to any of these, the ideas of the modernists liberated him from the academic manner that he had learned in Mexico.

When Rivera returned home, his art took an exhilarating new direction. He produced a flood of drawings representing the landscapes, people, legends, and history of his homeland. He conceived these as preparations for murals depicting contemporary life and social and political history. Like many of Rivera's sketches of the difficult lives of peasants in Mexico's deserts and jungles, *Mother and Child* expresses simple, sincere human emotion. It reflects the artist's respect for the dignity of the poor and his deep convictions as one of the country's most celebrated Communists.

—DA

MAN RAY
   American, 1890–1976
   Nancy Cunard, 1927
   Gelatin silver print
   3¼ × 2½ in. (8.3 × 6.4 cm)
   Eliza S. Paine Fund, 1987.80

From the beginning of his career in New York, Man Ray was associated with avant-garde art. After his move to Paris in 1921, he established himself as a talented Dada-Surrealist, creating dreamlike paintings and photographs. Using photography as a means of support, he became an outstanding advertising and portrait photographer.

   One of numerous celebrities who posed for Man Ray was Nancy Cunard (1896–1965), daughter of a California heiress and a famous shipping magnate. Counting many Surrealists among her friends, she was a member of London's radical literary group Blast and was the model for the main female character in Aldous Huxley's *Point Counter Point.* Like Man Ray, Cunard endeavored to change society's attitudes. She became an authority on black culture and fought for civil rights in America during the 1930s. For this tightly framed portrait she wears the African bracelets that she collected.   —SBJ

ARSHILE GORKY
American (born in Armenia), 1904–48
Painter and Model, 1931
Lithograph on cream wove paper
11¼ × 9⅞ in. (28.7 × 25.2 cm) image
Eliza S. Paine Fund, Sarah C. Garver Fund,
and Heald Foundation Fund, 1990.15

Gorky has been described as the last of the American Surrealists and the first Abstract Expressionist. A pioneer in the development of a distinctly American dialect of abstract art, this immigrant painter first worked in a Cubist style, profoundly indebted to Pablo Picasso. He then developed an emotionally charged abstract Surrealist manner and afterward a more lyrical, biomorphic abstraction based on the work of Joan Miró. In the late 1920s Gorky shared ideas with his friend Stuart Davis, who had recently returned to New York from Paris, where he had made a group of lithographs in modernist styles.

Davis probably introduced Gorky to lithography and to George C. Miller, a professional printer in New York who collaborated on several of Davis's prints.

Painter and Model closely reproduces the design of Gorky's oil painting *Blue Figure in Chair* (about 1930; private collection). Although the artist designated the print as one from an edition of twenty-five, just a handful of impressions are known today. This suggests that the impoverished young artist drew the stones himself and arranged with Miller to make a few prints, hoping to finish the edition when funds from the sale of the first lithographs allowed. Judging from the extreme rarity of this lithograph, it seems unlikely that the edition was ever completed.

—DA

WALKER EVANS
        American, 1903–75
        Street and Graveyard in Bethlehem,
        Pennsylvania, 1936
        Gelatin silver print
        6⅞ × 6⅜ in. (17.4 × 16.2 cm)
        Gift of Dr. and Mrs. Robert A. Johnson,
        1981.337

Evans emerged as one of America's leading documentary artists in the 1930s, when he worked for the Resettlement Administration (a federal agency that later became the Farm Security Administration), photographing social conditions in the United States. This view of Bethlehem, one of a series taken in eastern Pennsylvania, juxtaposes several compositional elements in an urban scene near the steel mills—workers' houses, a distant church, trolley tracks, and a graveyard across the street. The camera lens reveals that within the graveyard, which has fallen into neglect, individual monuments have been tended by the living.

Evans cropped his eight-by-ten-inch negative to create a compact, square composition. The photograph in its full rectangular format was reproduced in the artist's first book, *Walker Evans: American Photographs,* published in 1938 by the Museum of Modern Art in New York. Noted for his stark, realistic pictures from the Great Depression years, Evans influenced younger photographers like Robert Frank (born 1924), who traveled across the continent to make a parallel study of American society in the 1950s.

—SBJ

MARSDEN HARTLEY

American, 1877–1943
The Wave, 1940–41
Oil on masonite
30¼ × 40⅞ in. (76.8 × 103.8 cm)
Museum purchase, 1942.1

A highly original painter, Hartley belonged to the first generation of American artists who, in the 1910s, worked in abstraction. Like many of his most innovative American contemporaries, he was influenced during those years by European modern art, especially Cubism and German Expressionism. Although he painted both completely nonfigurative compositions and identifiable subjects in various phases of his career, Hartley always maintained a keen appreciation for the emotional impact of abstract forms.

The Wave is one of a group of late seascapes that Hartley painted in his native Maine. He captured the elemental force of the pounding sea through generalization of forms rather than through descriptive details: looming against the horizon are rising waves that will break momentarily across the band of foreground rock. Hartley's dynamic, rough brushwork delineating the ragged silhouette of the white water enhances the impression of nature's raw power.　　　—SES

MARGARET BOURKE-WHITE
American, 1904–71
*Moscow under Air Attack, Parachute Flare
Reflected in the Moscow River,* 1941
Gelatin silver print
9 ¹³⁄₁₆ × 13 ½ in. (24.9 × 34.3 cm)
Gift of the artist, 1971.20

Bourke-White, one of this century's outstanding photojournalists, began her career in 1929 as *Fortune* magazine's first photographer. Her work took her in the early 1930s to Russia, where she photographed the new industrial complexes and where she examined, through portraiture, the character of an emerging Soviet society. In World War II Bourke-White became the first woman to serve as a combat photographer. As a *Life* correspondent she returned to Russia before the Nazi invasion in June 1941 and was the only foreign photographer in Moscow when the air attacks started.

This long exposure, taken from the roof of the British Embassy during an air raid in August, depicts war in all its ferocity: a parachute flare drops behind star-topped towers into the Kremlin grounds, and Russian tracer bullets and bursting shells probe the night sky for attacking German aircraft.   —SBJ

GRACE HARTIGAN
American, born 1922
King of the Hill, 1950
Oil on canvas
67¼ × 48 in. (170.8 × 121.9 cm)
Sarah C. Garver Fund, 1971.114

Hartigan's canvases of the early 1950s reflect the influence of two older artists whose work early on helped define Abstract Expressionism. Jackson Pollock's rhythmic drip paintings and Willem de Kooning's energetic, expressionistic brushstrokes provided Hartigan with the freedom to explore an allover, gestural, abstract vocabulary. In *King of the Hill* lively, calligraphic lines weaving through areas of dense color flow off the edge of the canvas. This, coupled with the absence of a single focal point, creates a dynamic surface. The pure abstraction evident here constitutes a short episode in Hartigan's oeuvre. By 1952, while still maintaining an expressive, gestural style, she had introduced figurative elements into her work.   —DH

FRANZ KLINE
American, 1910–62
Spectre, 1956
Oil on canvas
65 × 50 in. (165.1 × 127 cm)
Gift of Mrs. John Woodman Higgins in
memory of her son, Carter Chapin Higgins,
1967.14

Kline was one of the original members of the Abstract Expressionists, a group of American artists centered in New York City who came to prominence by 1950. Also called the New York School, these painters sought a language of abstraction that was uniquely American and would represent their own emotional and spiritual states. Early in his career Kline worked in a gritty, figurative idiom, focusing on urban scenes. In 1950, encouraged by the gestural abstraction of fellow painters Jackson Pollock and Willem de Kooning, Kline developed his mature style—bold sweeps of black on a white ground applied with a house painter's brush. The dense image of *Spectre,* conveyed in vigorous strokes, confronts the viewer with the artist's characteristic aggressiveness and raw energy. —DH

ELLSWORTH KELLY
American, born 1923
Orange White, 1961
Oil on canvas
84⅛ × 60⅛ in. (213.6 × 152.7 cm)
Museum purchase, 1963.80

The art of Kelly followed in the wake of Abstract Expressionism and presaged the simplified format of Minimalism. Known as "hard-edge abstraction" because of the cleanly defined contours of abstract shapes, Kelly's work celebrates a belief in the primacy of form and the power of pure color. His paintings (like his sculpture and prints) are often distilled from what he observes in the real world—fragments of architecture, shadows, plant life, or the "space between things"—though the final image is abstract. The absence of visible brushstrokes or any trace of the artist's hand, along with the use of pure, flat, unmodulated color, results in anonymous, dispassionate, neutral surfaces.

Throughout Kelly's work there is an intriguing relationship between figure and ground: rather than seeming to exist on different planes, the two are often contiguous in a way that makes it difficult to distinguish one from the other. *Orange White* bears out this ambivalence; the swelling orange form and the white framing edge are locked into a single plane, where they coexist in dynamic tension.   —DH

TOM WESSELMANN
American, born 1931
Great American Nude #36, 1962
Enamel and polymer paint and collage
on composition board
48 × 60 in. (121.9 × 152.4 cm)
Museum purchase, 1965.393

Once strongly influenced by the Abstract Expressionist Willem de Kooning, Wesselmann developed a signature style with subject matter drawn from everyday life and mass culture. His works are rendered with the cool detachment of advertising imagery common to Pop Art. Wesselmann is best known for a series of nude women presented as American icons, which he began in 1961. Inspired by a dream about the words red, white, and blue, he titled the series *Great American Nude* and initially limited his palette primarily to those colors.

In *Great American Nude #36* Wesselmann created a pastiche of traditional subject matter by collaging photomechanically reproduced images of a near life-size reclining female figure, a landscape, and a still life onto the painting. These themes are updated by the artist's bold, flat painting style and the addition of commonplace materials such as fabric and fringe. The inclusion of a Matisse still life with oysters confirms the implicit sexual connotations of the woman's suggestive pose.

—DH

ROBERT RAUSCHENBERG
American, born 1925
Accident, 1963
Lithograph on cream wove paper
38⅝ × 27¼ in. (97.4 × 69.3 cm) image
Museum purchase through the National
Endowment for the Arts, 1977.9

Rauschenberg's distinctive style melds the collage and assemblage of Dada with the spontaneous, actively applied paint of the Abstract Expressionists. In his "combine" paintings of the 1950s an array of found objects are juxtaposed on conventional stretched canvas, which was afterward overpainted. The artist also appropriated images from magazines and newspapers, chemically transferring the ink from the printed page to his own drawings. During the 1960s he applied photomechanical techniques to capture the imagery of popular culture for his silkscreens and lithographs. When the large lithographic stone used for this print, which had taken Rauschenberg many hours to prepare, began to break under the pressure of the press, the artist insisted on continuing. The image evolved as the crevice between the two fractured halves widened. Thus an event that would normally have been a lithographer's tragedy was transformed into a creative triumph. The result affords a glimpse into both the printmaking process and the experience of twentieth-century life in America, so commonly affected by technology. This lithograph, afterward entitled *Accident,* has become one of the most enduring monuments in the history of American printmaking.   —DA

BRUCE DAVIDSON
    American, born 1933
    Untitled, 1966–68
    Gelatin silver print
    12⅝ × 16¹¹⁄₁₆ in. (32 × 42.3 cm)
    Museum purchase through the gift
    of Mrs. Joseph Goodhue, 1982.14

After graduating from the Rochester Institute of Technology, Davidson studied philosophy and graphic arts at Yale under Josef Albers, a former Bauhaus teacher. During a long career as a photojournalist, having joined the agency Magnum Photos in 1957, he has produced significant photo essays about such diverse subjects as teenagers at Coney Island, the Verrazano-Narrows Bridge under construction, and riders on the New York subway.

When Davidson went into New York City's Spanish Harlem in 1966 to photo-graph life on East 100th Street, someone said to him, "What you call the ghetto, I call my home." The artist did not forget these words as he took pictures during his two-year project. With an eight-by-ten-inch view camera, Davidson portrayed the hard reality of tenement life, yet he preserved the dignity and individuality of his subjects. This image was reproduced in his book *East 100th Street* (1970).   —SBJ

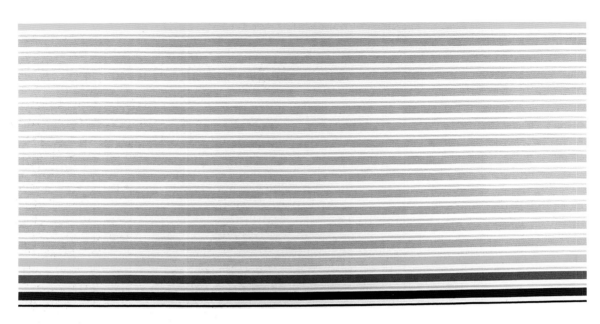

KENNETH NOLAND
American, born 1924
Lyre, 1967
Acrylic on canvas
102 × 196 in. (260 × 500 cm)
Gift of the Worcester Art Museum
Members' Council, 1975.664

The style of Noland's work, which falls under the rubrics Post-Painterly Abstraction and Color Field painting, is characterized by an ongoing investigation of color and structure. In contrast to the expressive gesture and content of Abstract Expressionism, his art is one in which color, freed from a descriptive or emotive function, is in itself a visual experience. By staining paint directly into unprimed canvas, the artist eliminates any surface incident that might detract from the painting's pristine quality or the sensation of pure color.

Noland characteristically employs a limited vocabulary of simple shapes, such as the repeating horizontal bands in *Lyre.* Not unlike the strings of the instrument of the painting's title, these stripes of alternating width and color, in concert with the white of the raw canvas, produce subtle optical vibrations.

—DH

LOUISE NEVELSON

American (born in Russia), 1900–1988
Black Garden Wall III, 1971
Painted wood and formica
H: 86 in. (218.4 cm) w: 44 in. (111.8 cm)
D: 7 in. (17.8 cm)
Sarah C. Garver Fund, 1976.42

As the title suggests, nature and architecture are closely allied in Nevelson's work. Her mysterious wall constructions, among the most original contributions to modern sculpture, are a synthesis of diverse influences. These assemblages wed elements from two significant early twentieth-century European movements: the clarity and precision of Constructivism and the fragmented forms and additive process of Cubism. In her desire to create an emotionally charged art, Nevelson was equally drawn to the powerful evocation of myth and ritual in Precolumbian art.

Black Garden Wall III is a relief sculpture composed of eight separate boxes organized into an irregular grid of myriad compartments filled with pieces of wood and discarded architectural fragments. To unify the disparate elements into a coherent composition, the entire work has been painted matte black—a neutral color that negates the articles' previous functions and transforms them into mysterious objects. As it absorbs light, Nevelson's dark, somber surface creates a theatrical play of light and shadow.   —DH

BEVERLY PEPPER
American, born 1924
Double Pyramid, 1971
Cor-Ten steel
H: 9 ft. (2.7 m) W: 23 ft. (7 m)
D: 25 ft. (7.6 m)
Museum purchase, funded by a gift from
the National Endowment for the Arts and
by an anonymous donor, 1972.112

Pepper, best known for her monumentally scaled public sculpture and ambitious earthworks, was trained as a painter. She switched to sculpture after a visit in 1960 to Angkor Wat, the ancient Cambodian temple complex. Within two years Pepper developed a friendship with the seminal American sculptor David Smith, whose welded steel constructions, fabricated in factories, had an early and important impact on her work.

Double Pyramid is akin to a group of Pepper's works from the early 1970s that reflects the influence of Minimalism in the use of industrial materials fashioned into spare, geometric forms. Made of Cor-Ten steel, an alloy that rusts naturally when exposed to the atmosphere, the two large-scale pyramidal shapes rise obliquely out of the ground and seem to defy gravity in their cantilevered stance. A dynamic tension created by this precarious balance is enhanced by the asymmetry of the forms and their subtly skewed disposition. The sculpture's apparent simplicity is deceptive; further examination reveals a complex relationship among its multiple planes. —DH

HARRY CALLAHAN
American, born 1912
Cape Cod, 1972
Gelatin silver print
9½ × 9¹¹⁄₁₆ in. (24.1 × 24.7 cm)
Austin S. Garver Fund, 1977.31

Callahan, who was born in Detroit, has been active since the 1940s as both a photographer and a teacher. Drawn to the commonplace, he follows his intuition in selecting subjects to photograph in the natural landscape and urban settings. Callahan's distinctive images of the everyday world fuse two traditions—the American sharp-focus documentary style dating from the 1930s and the abstract, geo-metric photography of László Moholy-Nagy, with whom he worked in Chicago. Unlike the documentary photographers Paul Strand and Walker Evans, Callahan does not invest his imagery with a social message.

This beach scene stands out as a key picture in Callahan's extensive Cape Cod series from the early 1970s. His interest in space and viewpoint is evident in the way he employed his camera lens to direct the viewer's attention outward to the horizon and downward to the lower right. The diagonal line of the beach gives the composition its arresting dramatic emphasis.   —SBJ

ELIZABETH MURRAY
American, born 1940
Undoing, 1989–90
Etching and lithograph on white
wove paper
28 15/16 × 22 15/16 in. (73.6 × 58.4 cm) sheet
Sarah C. Garver Fund, 1991.96

Murray is known for distinctive abstractions of everyday objects, which she invests with private meaning. Her multilayered prints are analogous to her paintings, often constructed of several shaped canvases joined together. *Undoing* is made from three pieces of paper, hand torn to form organic shapes and laid, askew, one on top of the other. Printed in nine colors from as many plates, the work reveals a complexity of successive layers of colors. A welter of gestural marks and lines—vestiges of the artist's early assimilation of Abstract Expressionism—combines with cartoonish images recalling Pop Art: a foot, a gesticulating hand, and two bottles from which liquid flows, all emerging from tubes resembling limbs or intestines. Both abstract elements and representational forms seem to be pulled into a vortex toward the hole running through all three sheets in narrowing concentric circles. The title appears to relate to this uncontrollable spiral movement and to the connected, yet dislocated, forms.   —AD

CATALOGUE AUTHORS

AD   Annette Dixon, formerly Assistant Curator of Prints and Drawings, is currently Curator of Western Art at the University of Michigan Art Museum.

DA   David Acton is Curator of Prints and Drawings.

DH   Donna Harkavy is Curator of Contemporary Art.

EdeSS   Elizabeth de Sabato Swinton is Curator of Asian Art.

JAW   James A. Welu is Director of the Worcester Art Museum and Curator of European Art.

MPL   Mary Pax Lenny received her M.A. from the Latin American Institute of the University of Texas at Austin.

SBJ   Stephen B. Jareckie is Curator of Photography and Museum Archivist.

SES   Susan E. Strickler is Director of Curatorial Affairs and Curator of American Art.

SHA   Susan Heuck Allen received her Ph.D. from Brown University and has taught ancient art at Smith College and at Clark, Tufts, and Yale universities.

VCR   Virginia Chieffo Raguin, a medieval scholar, is Chair of the Department of Visual Arts at the College of the Holy Cross.

BIBLIOGRAPHY

Acton, David. *A Spectrum of Innovation: Color in American Printmaking, 1890–1960.* New York and London: W. W. Norton & Company, 1990.

Art through Fifty Centuries: From the Collections of the Worcester Art Museum. Worcester, 1948.

Buhler, Kathryn C. *American Silver: From the Colonial Period through the Early Republic in the Worcester Art Museum.* Worcester, 1979.

Dresser, Louisa, ed. *European Paintings in the Collection of the Worcester Art Museum.* 2 vols. Worcester: Worcester Art Museum in cooperation with the University of Massachusetts Press, 1974.

Findly, Ellison Banks. *From the Courts of India: Indian Miniatures in the Collection of the Worcester Art Museum.* Worcester, 1981.

A Handbook to the Worcester Art Museum. Worcester, 1973.

Jareckie, Stephen B. *The Early Republic: Consolidation of Revolutionary Goals.* Worcester, 1976.

Reutlinger, Dagmar E. *The Colonial Epoch in America.* Worcester, 1975.

Riggs, Timothy A. *The Second Fifty Years: American Art, 1826–1876.* Worcester, 1976.

Strickler, Susan E. *American Portrait Miniatures: The Worcester Art Museum Collection.* Worcester, 1989.

Strickler, Susan E., ed. *American Traditions in Watercolor: The Worcester Art Museum Collection.* New York: Abbeville Press, 1987.

Steinberg, Norma S. *Monstrosities and Inconveniences: Works by George Cruikshank from the Worcester Art Museum.* Worcester, 1986.

Additional references to individual works of art and to portions of the collection appear in the following museum publications:

Worcester Art Museum Annual Report, 1899–1988

Worcester Art Museum Bulletin, vols. 1–25, 1910–35

Worcester Art Museum News Bulletin, vols. 1–36, 1935–71

Worcester Art Museum Bulletin, New Series, vols. 1–7, 1971–78

Worcester Art Museum Journal, vols. 1–8, 1977–86